With
My Best Wishes
To

Eric Mohring
a
Future millionaire

Fred J. Young

HOW TO
GET RICH
AND
STAY RICH

HOW TO
GET RICH
AND
STAY RICH

Fred J. Young

FREDERICK FELL PUBLISHERS, INC., NEW YORK

For information address:

Frederick Fell Publishers, Inc.
386 Park Avenue South
New York, New York 10016

Library of Congress Catalog Card Number: 82-83771
International Standard Book Number: 0-8119-0491-1

MANUFACTURED IN THE UNITED STATES OF AMERICA

Designed by Michael U. Polvere

1 2 3 4 5 6 7 8 9 0

Published simultaneously in Canada by Fitzhenry & Whiteside, Limited, Toronto

DEDICATION

THIS book is dedicated to the airlines—to United, American, TWA, Delta, Eastern, Northwest, North Central, Braniff, and Ozark—because it was written while I waited for or rode on their airplanes. My many hours airborne came as I traveled around the country making speeches on *How to Get Rich and Stay Rich*.

CONTENTS

Foreword

By Beryl W. Sprinkel

YES, Fred Young is for real. He is vice-president of the Harris Trust and Savings Bank of Chicago and has been a dear friend and colleague of mine for twenty-five years. Throughout his banking career he has remained an enthusiastic, hard-working, and productive employee in the field of investments. For fifteen years he was a security analyst and developed a well-deserved reputation for counseling customers and fellow employees on financial and personal matters. His empathy, his friendliness, his self-confidence, and his Tennessee horse sense enabled him to build countless friendships throughout Chicago and, more recently, throughout the entire United States.

If he has a fault, it is excessive dedication to his work to the detriment of leisure. I once accused him of having no avocation, but he set me straight by assuring me that his consuming hobby was cashing dividend checks and clipping interest coupons!

Fred hit his stride about 1965 when he was given responsibility for developing, selling, and servicing the Institutional Investment Service, which counsels such other professional investors as trust departments, insurance companies, and mutual funds. Mainly through his efforts this service now has more subscribers than any similar service in the country—over five-hundred satisfied customers. In addition to distributing the Harris Bank's research on securities and economics, Fred writes a spritely and widely read monthly commentary on the current investment scene, making inherently dull financial and economic analysis relevant and interesting. He also sells and services a popular fixed income service and an individual stock advisory service. In addition he is witty, articulate, and much-sought-after speaker, especially on the subject of *"How to Get Rich and Stay Rich!"*

For several years I have urged Fred to write this book. I am convinced that his wide investment knowledge and experience deserve an even larger audience. If you read and adopt the principles that Fred had developed over a lifetime of experience and reflection, you too will have an opportunity to enjoy the benefits of well-managed financial independence and security. Even if you decide you prefer to "live it up," I assure you that you will enjoy reading this book. Yes, there is only one Fred Young—but the principles that he lives by can become your own.

Beryl W. Sprinkel

Preface

My Qualifications for Writing This Book

FOR twenty-five years I have worked in the Trust Department of the Harris Trust and Savings Bank in Chicago, Illinois. Most of my time during this period has been spent helping rich people (1) stay rich and (2) get richer.

The Harris Bank at the time of this writing has the ninth largest Trust Department in the United States with more than $10 billion under management. These assets belong to wealthy individuals or institutions of all kinds, including pension plans, profit-sharing plans, hospital endowment funds, college endowment funds, foundations, and others.

During these twenty-five years of working with rich people, I have made a number of observations about getting rich, being rich, and staying rich and about the difference wealth makes. I am delighted to share these observations with you in this book. I hope these observations will be an inspiration to you to manage your own financial affairs better. I am convinced that happiness is good personal financial management.

I do want to include a disclaimer here. This book is not all-inclusive on the matter of how to get rich and stay rich. It includes only my personal observations on the matter. I am sure most bank trust officers or other professional money managers could add to it. I doubt, however, that any would eliminate anything from it. I firmly believe everything that I have included here.

Fred J. Young

HOW TO
GET RICH
AND
STAY RICH

CHAPTER I

In The Beginning

I GREW up on a farm near Whitesburg, Tennessee, but when I moved to Chicago many years ago, I figured that people up North would not know anything about Whitesburg, so I adopted the next biggest town to be from—Bulls Gap, Tennessee.

Now what does this have to do with my views about getting rich and staying rich? Plenty. There were no rich people in either Whitesburg or Bulls Gap when I was there. In fact, I never knew a rich person until I came to Chicago. While in law school at the University of Missouri in the late 1930s, I carefully avoided taking the course in Trusts and Estates because I assumed I would never know anyone wealthy enough to have an estate problem.

Since my background was so far removed from rich people, I was completely fascinated when I found myself constantly dealing with them at the Harris Bank.

CHAPTER II

Getting From There to Here

HOW does a farm boy from East Tennessee get to be an adviser to the rich in Chicago, Illinois? This is a question I get not infrequently. Perhaps you, too, would be interested in knowing. So I will tell you as briefly as possible.

As a youngster I never liked working on that farm. The crops were never right because it was always too hot or too cold, or too wet or too dry. If we had a good season, then prices would collapse from oversupply. As I hoed that corn on the side of the hill, I kept thinking to myself, "There has got to be a better way to make a living than this." One day my father had an occasion to consult a young lawyer in Morristown, Tennessee. He was impressed with this lawyer, and in telling my mother about him he commented, "That young lawyer knows everything." That did it. I would be a lawyer when I grew up because I would like to know everything.

When I got out of law school in 1941, the draft board was looking for me. It found me on December 8, 1941, the day Congress declared war on most of the world. I was working in the Accounting Department of TVA in Knoxville at the time. On December 9 I volunteered for the navy as an apprentice seaman. I returned to the office and told my boss at TVA what I had done. The word quickly spread throughout that big office that a brave young man in the Travel Section had volunteered for the Navy. "Isn't he wonderful?" the girls all said. "It is young men like

17

him who make this nation great,'' they said. The next day the married ladies started coming by and saying things like, ''I told my husband what you did. He said if he weren't married, he would do just what you did.'' Well, most of them got a chance to do just that later. I graciously accepted all this praise without mentioning to anyone that I had my draft notice in my pocket.

After nine months of being moved around in the Navy from Great Lakes, Illinois, to Corpus Christi, Texas, to New Orleans, Louisiana, I got assigned to the Legal Medicine Section of the Bureau of Medicine and Surgery in Washington, D. C. I reported there in September 1942 to a Commander Benjamin E. Irwin, one of the greatest gentlemen I have ever known. Commander Irwin said, ''Young, we do not expect much of you for the first six months. It will take that long for you to figure out what we are doing here.'' I said, ''You mean I will be here six months?'' I hadn't been anywhere in the Navy more than three months. He said, ''It all depends on how you work out. If you work out well, you will be here longer than that. If you don't, you won't.'' I guess I worked out well; I stayed there the remainder of the war.

When I got out of the Navy in 1946 I took a job with the Veterans Administration in a legal capacity, and they transferred me to Chicago. In 1947 I went to Fort Scott, Kansas, and married my wife, Grace Woodward, brought her to Chicago, and sent her to an employment agency. They directed her to a well-known brokerage house called Glore, Forgan & Company to be Philip Moncreiff's secretary. Mr. Moncreiff was in charge of Glore, Forgan's Investment Advisory Division, managing investments for rich clients. My wife frequently worked until nine or ten o'clock at night preparing Moncreiff's accounts and typing his letters. While she worked, I would go to Mr. Moncreiff's office on the fortieth floor of the Field Building and read all the investment material on his desk, including his investment letters to clients.

As a result, I became fascinated with the investment business. I had always wanted to own everything in sight and had been buying stocks with any money I could raise, but this was the first time I realized a person could get paid a living wage in the investment business. Somehow it had never occurred to me that a poor man could make a good living helping rich people get richer. Nobody told me about that when I was on the farm.

In early 1952 I went to Mr. Moncreiff and told him I wanted to do what he was doing. I had definitely decided that this was the thing for me instead of law. How could I get into this business?

Mr. Moncreiff observed that I had no experience in the investment business, that I would not be worth much of anything to any employer until I got some experience. Then he said that if I was really serious about doing this, I should go to either the Northern Trust or the Harris Bank and get a job in the Investment Research Department. He said those were the two best organized, most effective such departments in Chicago. He advised me not to quibble over salary, that banks do not pay good salaries, but that after I got three years' experience, if things worked out well for me, then I would have investment experience that I could sell up and down LaSalle Street if my pay at the bank was not satisfactory.

So I went to the Northern Trust, but they showed a marked lack of enthusiasm for me. I then went to the Harris Bank and, oddly enough, they were interested. But I almost blew it. William C. Norby was head of the Investment Research Department at the Harris. At that time he had never worked anyplace but at the Harris Bank and was the most dedicated company man I had ever met. He didn't think there was any suitable place to work except at the Harris.

It was Mr. Norby who asked me what I had in mind in the way of a salary. I had anticipated this question and had what I thought was a good answer. I said, "Mr. Norby, I fully realize banks don't pay very good salaries. . . ." He raised up in his chair, got pink behind the ears, and interrupted me with, "There is where you are wrong. You will find salaries at the Harris Bank comparable to salaries in industry anywhere." I did not get an opportunity to complete my statement that I had decided I wanted

19

to work in his Research Department and didn't want salary to be a determining factor.

I was making $7,600 a year at the Veterans Administration at the time. Two weeks later I got a letter from Fred Stone, head of the Personnel Department, stating that the Harris was prepared to offer me employment with a starting salary of $4,500 a year. I wrote back that I would take it starting April 1, 1952, which I did. About the middle of April my wife decided she should see a doctor. Something wasn't right. Sure enough, she was pregnant. She had to quit her job, and we had to buy a house suitable for raising a family. Our family income went down by 67 percent in 1952. If I had known two weeks earlier that our son would be joining us I would not have had the nerve to take that salary cut and assume the uncertainty of starting over in a new career.

But it all worked out well. I have thoroughly enjoyed my twenty-five years of working with rich people at the Harris Bank. I find rich people very fascinating. They can do so many things poor people can't do. They can also get into all kinds of interesting difficulties that poor people can't afford. I want to share with you in this book my observations on getting rich, being rich, staying rich, and what difference it makes.

CHAPTER III

Anyone Can Get Rich Who Wants to Badly Enough

ANYONE who wants to badly enough can get rich. This is a rather blunt statement, and I firmly believe it is true, so I will repeat it. Any reasonably healthy American of normal intelligence (or less) can make himself rich under our free enterprise system if he wants to badly enough and starts early enough in life.

Then why aren't we all rich? There is a certain percentage of our population who do not care to be rich. At least, that is not their primary goal in life. I am talking about Salvation Army people, religious workers, some teachers, social workers—people whose primary interest is in serving their fellow man, not in accumulating great wealth. And I submit that we are fortunate that we have these people in our midst. Without them, the world that you and I live in would not be a fit place in which to live.

A much larger percentage of our population do not realize early enough in life that it is possible for them to get rich under our system. By the time they discover that they can, it is too late; time has run out on them. I do not mean to imply that only the young can get rich. Not at all. There are too many examples of well-known people who made their fortunes after retiring at age sixty-five. Who hasn't heard of Colonel Sanders and how he financed his Kentucky Fried Chicken on his social security checks? Or Arthur Vining Davis who made a big fortune in Florida real estate after he retired from Alcoa? Examples of fortunes made after retirement are numerous, but my advice to you is not to wait until you are retired to seek your fortune. It is too risky. You are far more likely to make it if you start early in life; the earlier the better. I will say more about this later.

The vast majority of the American people would love to be rich "but not that much." The term "not that much" is something I learned from my teenaged son a few years ago, but I think it is a very expressive term. He was a capable, smart kid, but never on the honor roll. One day while examining his report card, I asked him if he wouldn't like to be on the honor roll, and he answered, "Sure, Dad, but not that much." You know what he meant. That took extra work and sacrifice, and he didn't want the honor that much. And that is the way with most Americans. They would like to be rich, but that takes too much effort, and this brings me to my second observation.

CHAPTER IV

All Riches Involve a Sacrifice

IN THE case of every rich person or wealthy family that I have dealt with over the past twenty-five years, someone made the sacrifice of spending less than he (or she) earned and invested the difference in something that went up in value and made him or her rich. Maybe some people, somewhere, sometime, got rich without making any kind of a sacrifice, but I have never run across them.

The sacrifice may have been made by the rich man (or woman), or by his father, or grandfather, or great grandfather, or uncle, or friend, or someone else. I suppose if an oil well pops up in the back forty, the sacrifice isn't very great, but then someone had to save up the money to buy the back forty in the first place.

Most of the great fortunes I know about were started by someone who worked long hours, scrimped and saved, and made unbelievable sacrifices to get the fortune started.

I am convinced that the good Lord did not look down upon this earth and say, "You and you and you and your families shall be forever rich. You and you and you and your families shall be forever poor." That is not the way it happened at all. The families that are rich are rich because someone did something that made them rich.

CHAPTER V

What Constitutes Being Rich Varies Greatly From One Individual To Another

ECONOMIC background seems to color one's idea of what constitutes being rich. Some of my contacts with relatively modest means feel they are very well off, while others with far more money than they could ever spend feel they are practically destitute.

I mentioned before that my wife grew up in Kansas. She likes living in Chicago except during the winters, which she finds too long and too cold. Even the summers here are too cold for her. Her idea of a good vacation is two weeks in Kansas in August. So every year she goes back to Kansas in August for her vacation. A few years ago she and the children were returning from their vacation in Kansas on the Santa Fe Chief. I went down to the Dearborn Street Station to meet them, and as so often happened, the train was quite late. This was the hottest day of the year, and when it gets hot in Chicago, the Dearborn Street Station seems to get hotter than anyplace else.

All the trains appeared to be late in departing as well as arriving, and the station was crowded with people. There was one large, middle-aged lady whose voice carried well above all the noise. And she talked incessantly. I noticed that she kept moving around because the people she talked to kept getting up and moving. Finally, she was seated next to me, and I learned her story. She had come to the station about three hours before her train was scheduled to leave for Evansville, Indiana, because it was absolutely essential that she be on that train. Her brother-in-law had died in Evansville, and her sister needed her to help manage her affairs. Her brother-in-law had been a stingy old miser who never gave her sister anything, but now he was dead, and her sister was rich. She must get down there to counsel the sister on managing her wealth. I asked how much money her brother-in-law had left her sister. Her answer came in a very loud voice: "Fifty thousand dollars!"

Now I admit $50,000 is a lot of money, especially if it is yours. But I doubt that most people would consider having $50,000 as being rich. It so happens that a few days after this incident one of the vice-presidents of the Harris Bank brought a lady to see me because she had a real problem. She simply could not get along on the $36,000-a-year income from her investments. Something had to be done to get her more income. Could I help her?

At first I wasn't very sympathetic. Anyone who can't get along on $36,000 a year doesn't seem worthy of much sympathy. But then her story unfolded. She was a recent widow. This was her second husband. Her more than $800,000 came from her first husband and her father. She and her second husband had a prenuptial agreement that what was hers was hers and what was his was his. This is not too unusual and is a good way to keep harmony among the children of each. He was the senior partner in a big law firm, and his take was $100,000 a year, which they had been living up to completely. So this couple had been spending her $36,000 income, his $100,000 salary, plus the income he got from his investments. Granted, a lot of this went for taxes but still they were living well. Then all of a sudden his $100,000 stopped, and she was faced with reducing to a $36,000 level.

I suggested that she would have to economize. She said she already had economized. I asked what she had done. She said she had laid off the chauffeur. I observed that she was paying $1,200 per month rent on her apartment and suggested she move to a smaller apartment. She said she couldn't do that because she had to have room for her cook and her maid. "But you wouldn't need a live-in maid if you were in a smaller apartment," said I. "My good man," she said in exasperation, "you simply do not understand. I am seventy-two years old and never in my life have I spent even one night alone. I must have people with me at all times. I cannot stand being alone." See why she was poverty stricken on an income of $36,000 a year while the other lady was definitely rich with $50,000 in assets? Obviously, these ladies had very different economic backgrounds that influenced their attitudes about how well off they were.

"Am I wealthy?" This is a question I get frequently in my work at the Harris Bank. It comes in different wordings, but the meaning is always the same. Sometimes people will come to me and say. "Mr. Young, I know the Harris Bank manages money for wealthy people only. Here is what I have. Do I have enough to justify an account in your Trust Department?" Isn't he asking if we consider him to be wealthy?

Sometimes a customer or a prospective customer will outline to me what he has and then ask how his assets would compare with the other accounts we manage. Would he be a big account or a small account for us? In effect, "How do I compare with your wealthy clients?"

Sometimes the customer will simply say, "Do you consider me rich," or "Do you consider me wealthy?" A few years ago the bank received a letter from a Catholic priest in response to an ad we ran for municipal bonds we had for sale. Our Bond Department wasn't sure what to do with the letter, so they sent it to me.

In the letter the priest outlined in great detail all his assets; then he listed a number of questions:

1. Am I wealthy?
2. Should I retire as a priest?
3. If I retire, can I get along on what I have?
4. If I retire, should I move to New York City?
5. If I move to New York City, should I buy a house or rent an apartment?

27

I recognized this as a serious letter. This gentleman wanted to talk to someone about his personal affairs. I didn't know that Catholic priests were ever wealthy, but this one was. So I wrote him a serious answer. I said, "Yes, Father, you are wealthy. Yes, you should retire as a priest. (I am a Protestant and just couldn't resist a small blow for our side.) Yes, you can live on what you have. No, you should not move to New York City. You should move to Chicago, then you could do your banking at the Harris Trust and Savings Bank."

This gentleman was so appreciative of all the good advice I gave him that he came all the way to Chicago to thank me. But he still moved to New York City.

Here was a straightforward question. "Am I wealthy?" Well, are you wealthy? How do you know whether you are wealthy? In March 1976 the Conference Board, in an interesting and detailed report entitled "The National Wealth of the United States" by Dr. John W. Kendrich with Dr. Kyu Sik Lee and Jean Lomask, estimated the national wealth of the United States, as of the beginning of 1976, at $5.7 trillions. There were 214.4 million people in the United States at that time, so this averages out at $26,511 for each man, woman, and child in the country. Thus, if you have a net worth of less than $26,511, you are a drag on the system. You are below the national average and pretty clearly not rich. People in some undeveloped countries of the world think all Americans are rich, but I doubt that the readers of this book would accept this as being the case. In 1983 I checked with the Conference Board to see if they had updated these estimates. They had not. Obviously inflation alone would raise these figures by 50% or more.

I am going to let you answer your own question as to whether you are rich now or what it would take to make you feel that you are rich. I am convinced that your own attitude about what makes a person rich will, like the attitudes of the two ladies discussed earlier, have a lot to do with your answer.

Although being poor is not a part of the subject of this book, I am equally convinced that the perception that one is poor is also a matter of attitude. Neither my family nor our neighbors had any money to speak of when I was growing up in East Tennessee, but we certainly did not consider ourselves poor. In fact, my parents would have been highly insulted if anyone had told them we were poor people. We just didn't have much money. Other than that, we were always in great shape. Our small Methodist Church was so poor that we had preaching services only on the fifth Sunday of the month. Our circuit riding preacher had regular assignments at better paying churches on regular Sundays and was available for our church only in those months that had a fifth Sunday. Yet our church always pushed hard to increase "our benevolences." I have often wondered what the recipients of those benevolences looked like.

CHAPTER VI

There Are Only Three Ways To Get Rich

1. INHERIT IT. If you can see that you are going to inherit it, then you have it made. You can skip to the part of this book about staying rich. Someone else has already made the sacrifice of spending less than they earned to create this wealth for you. You should be grateful. You didn't have anything to do about it; your ancestry is completely beyond your control. You are fortunate indeed.

2. Marry it. This is an area in which you do have some control. This is something you can work on, but you have to get started on it before you get involved with some poor person. This can be quite a project, and I have seen both men and women work this approach to wealth quite effectively. I see nothing wrong with it. I grew up in an area and at a time when most people, boys and girls, firmly believed that the Good Lord made someone especially for them. Growing up for these young people was largely a search for their "intended." Well, if your intended, when you find him or her, happens to have a lot of money, you should graciously accept the situation. Don't fight it.

3. If you are not going to inherit it, and you have already blown the chance for wealth through marriage, then you have only one chance left to get rich. You spend less than you earn

and invest the difference in something that you think will increase in value and make you rich.

What should you invest in? Most rich people I know got rich from investments in one or more of the following:

a. Real estate
b. Own their own business
c. Common stocks
d. Savings accounts (thanks to the magic of compound interest rates)

REAL ESTATE AS AN INVESTMENT

Of all the rich people I know, more of them got rich from the ownership of real estate than any other single way. What kind of real estate? All kinds: farmland, commercial property, apartment houses, hotels, even single-family residences. Where? All over the country. When? Years ago, not long ago, and recently.

Is this a sure way to richness? Not at all. I also know a number of people who lost their shirts in real estate deals. Also, numerous large corporations have made headlines over the past few years with huge real estate losses. So what is the secret of getting rich in real estate? Frankly, I don't know, but my associate, John Alexander, who has had some experience in this area, says there are three essentials for making it in real estate: (1) location, (2) location, and (3) location. And how do you pick the right location for your real estate investment? It seems to be an inborn ability that some people have, plus a lot of luck. In many cases, the right choice is pure happenstance. In short, some people seem to have it and some don't.

I have observed that people who are intent on making a killing quick in real estate tend to be the ones who have the bad luck and end up losing their investment. The ones who are successful tend to be in no hurry. They have plenty of time. They will be there when the right location pays off.

A gentleman came to see me a few years ago about rearranging his investments to produce more income. He was in the process of retiring and did not want to lower his standard of living. He had stocks and bonds of a value that would make most people feel very wealthy indeed. At the end of our discussion I asked him what business he was in. He said he was a glue salesman. I remarked that selling glue must be an awfully good business if he'd made all that money. He said the glue business gave him a good living, but that he did not make this money selling glue. "Do you want to know how I made this money?" he asked. Of course, I said "Yes." So he took off his overcoat, sat back down, and began.

Back in 1940 he and his wife had two small sons. He and his wife had both grown up on farms, and they thought it would be nice if their boys could grow up on a farm. So they went way out west of Chicago and bought a farm. Their idea was that if they could just get their money back out of the farm when the last boy left for college, they would consider this a successful venture. (In 1940 farmland in general was still below its 1919 level, so the idea of getting their money back was a fairly optimistic expectation at that time.)

Well, in the mid 1950s the Illinois Toll Road Commission built a toll road right by their farm. About the time the last boy entered college, a gentleman showed up who wanted to buy their farm. He wanted to build houses on it. Today a good part of Hoffman Estates, Illinois, a city of 37,500, is built on their farm, and that was where he got all his money.

Happenstance? Luck? It certainly was not planning. He had no intention of making money in real estate, and that was the case of many wealthy people I know who made it big in real estate.

I tend to run across two types of real estate owners in my work here at the Harris Bank. Those who own real estate, especially apartment houses, inside the city of Chicago tend to be an unhappy group. Real estate taxes, union problems, vandalism, tenant demands, changing neighborhoods, and the like are driving them up the wall. They want out badly, some at any price, just to disassociate themselves from the problems. There may be happy real estate owners (other than home owners) inside Chicago, but with one exception, I have not met any of them.

On the other hand, the real estate owners of any kind outside Chicago in northern Illinois are a very happy group today. Farmland values have skyrocketed, and the owners have become very wealthy. Throughout the area, shopping centers and housing developments have sprung up right on the farms. A farmer friend of mine bought a farm six years ago at $400 an acre and sold it recently for $3,000 an acre. What did he do with it or to it during those six years? Nothing. He just held it and paid taxes on it, and it went up in value because a big corporation wanted that particular parcel for commercial use. This farmer had no plans to make a profit like that. Actually, he bought the farm to keep from paying capital gains taxes on another piece of farmland he was forced to sell to the interstate highway authority. I mentioned to this friend that he is the smartest investor I know. He repled, "Oh, no. I am not a smart investor. Haven't you heard the old saying that the dumbest farmer picks up the biggest potatoes?"

"Hot tip" information about making money in real estate invariably advocates maximum use of leverage—borrow as much money as possible. "Use the lenders money, not your own," say the brochures. But the people I know who have made it big in real estate used little or no debt. They paid cash. Maybe there are some who use debt successfully, but I have not met them.

One customer of the Harris Bank is worth at least $10 million, mostly made in real estate. No debts. In fact, he has over $800,000 in the Harris Bank Savings Department alone. He is in a maximum 70 percent tax bracket, but does not believe in owning municipal or tax-free bonds. He says he is pleased to be able to pay huge income taxes because our free enterprise system has made it possible for him to amass great wealth. Isn't he unusual? And he made most of it by paying cash for real estate. Where did he get the cash? Two sources: (1) the practice of law, and (2) pyramiding the income from his real estate investments. With the income from his first apartment hotel, he bought another, and the income from the two soon enabled him to buy another and another. The more apartment hotels he bought, the more income they produced; and the more income they produced, the more apartment hotels he bought. No wonder he is rich.

I have frequently run into big failures in real estate. They have invariably been people who were overextended with debt. When interest rates went up, as they did dramatically in 1974, such people could not pay the higher rates and were wiped out. I am not saying that you should not follow the conventional wisdom and borrow money to make money in real estate. I am saying that the people I know who made it big in real estate, and kept it, made it with their own money and not with borrowed money. Maybe somebody, somewhere, made it big in real estate by using borrowed money, but I have not yet met him.

Would the Harris Bank customer who made $10 million in real estate be worth $100 million or more today if he had borrowed all he could? Maybe so. Maybe not. Maybe he would have lost everything when interest rates skyrocketed. He is not interested in finding out. He likes it with no debts. He sleeps well at night. He considers the difference between $10 million and $100 million to be insignificant, but the difference between $10 million and no millions to be very, very important to him.

There are many notorious cases of big corporations with plenty of financial strength, either their own money or in good borrowing power, that have lost millions in real estate over the past few years. Who among you has not read in the papers about the Larwin Division of CNA Financial Corp. that lost about $80 million in 1974 from its real estate activities? The huge losses in real estate of IT&T's Levitt subsidiary are also well known, as are poor Boise Cascade's real estate developments that lost them about $78 million in 1971. This is big money lost in real estate by people with a lot of expertise and financial clout. Think how bad it can be for the little guy with limited financial resources.

So my conclusion would be (1) buy your real estate in the right location and I hope you have good ideas on location, (2) pay cash for it so you are never at the mercy of the lenders, and (3) have patience while you are waiting for oil or something to be found under it or for a housing development or shopping center to spring up on it. I fully realize that my exhortation to pay cash for your real estate is contrary to the conventional wisdom, but this book is based on my observations and not necessarily the conventional wisdom. The people I know who made it big in real estate did it with cash. The people I know who got wiped out in real estate were overextended with debt.

YOUR OWN BUSINESS

The second largest number of wealthy people I deal with became rich through their own business. I am sure some of our loan officers could write a book about people who went broke operating their own business, but people who are broke seldom show up in our Trust Department. We only see the successful ones, and the success stories are legion.

Did you ever hear of a rich garbage collector? Well, we have lots of them around Chicago now. Of course, they do not refer to themselves as garbage collectors. They say they are in the "solid waste disposal business." These people operated for years as small businessmen performing the valuable function of getting rid of waste, and they were paid a reasonable fee for this service. They managed their businesses well, plowing their earnings into more and more equipment that increased their efficiency and profits. Then along came a company called Waste Management, Inc., located in Oak Brook, Illinois. The founders of this company had the idea that they would acquire these independent operators, provide additional financial support, and computerize the growing business into a growth industry. It worked.

Many solid waste disposal people sold their businesses to Waste Management, Inc., a publicly held company, for anywhere from a few hundred thousand dollars to over $10 million.

This is all spelled out in Waste Management's prospectuses, including who got what, so I am not breaching any confidences here.

The point is that if self-employed people can make millions in the lowly business of getting rid of waste material, think of all of the more exotic ways to make a million in this huge economy of ours. Since many of the rich customers in the Harris's Trust Department became rich through the successful operation of their own businesses, I have to conclude that this is a good way to get rich.

COMMON STOCKS

Ownership of common stocks is a neat, convenient way for all of us to participate in the benefits of our free enterprise system to the full extent of our individual ability to do so. This is great. It does not take the big commitment that is invariably required of real estate investments; nor does it take the management ability that is always required in running your own business.

Few people have made money in the stock market over the past ten years because the market, as measured by the Dow Jones averages, is about where it was ten years ago. And there have been long periods like this before when stocks did nothing. But there have also been long periods when stocks went up sharply. We have a number of customers in our Trust Department who are rich today because they held stocks that went up in value. In fact, I would say that the ownership of common stocks has been the third most frequent means of attaining great wealth among the rich people I know.

Requirements For Successful Investing In Common Stocks

Investing in common stock is not a sure way to riches, however. My experience in dealing with investors over the past twenty-five years leads me to the conclusion that successful common stock investors have specific standard requirements:

Some Money

Although a successful investor needs some money, not much money is required to get started. Stocks are sold by the share, and some cost less than one dollar a share. So, technically, you would need less than a dollar, plus commission costs, to get started as a stock holder. From a practical standpoint you need more than a dollar to keep your commission costs in a reasonable proportion to your potential returns. Nevertheless, don't hesitate to start out small as an investor in common stocks. There is nothing wrong with buying in odd lots, which means less than one-hundred shares. If you wait until you can buy in round lots of one-hundred shares at a time, you may never get started because of the temptation to spend the money for consumer items.

I bought my first stock in October 1946 right after the big market drop in August and September 1946. My purchase was thirteen shares of General Motors at $48 a share. This cost me about $650 including brokers commissions. Why thirteen shares? That was all the money I could spare at the time, and after reading about stocks for several years, I had decided the time had come for me to get started.

I was working for the Veterans Administration in Washington, D.C., at the time. And this was the biggest deal I had ever pulled until then. I had never written a check for as much as $650 before. I was anxious to tell someone about it. So I went back to work and told one of my more sophisticated associates that I had decided that the way to get ahead in the world was to spend less than you earn and invest the difference in something that will go up. He thought that was awfully funny and yelled for the other guys to gather around and hear the great truth that this young man had discovered. Then he said, "Tell us, Young, what did you buy?" I told them thirteen shares of General Motors. They all thought that was the funniest thing they had ever heard. "Young has invested his money in General Motors, the most mature company in the nation, and he thinks that will make him rich. Isn't that funny?"

I took a lot of ribbing from my older and more knowledgeable associates in the office about this investment. One day I asked one of them to go for a walk with me up Constitution Avenue after lunch. Another of the guys interrupted and said, "Don't be taking walks with Young. He just wants to watch the Buicks go by. He thinks he is making a profit on each one." He was right. I did watch for new GM cars, and I did feel that I was a part owner in the enterprise.

Well, if I had held my General Motors stock until the end of 1982, I would have had seventy-eight shares as a result of two-for-one and three-for-one stock splits. These seventy-eight shares had a market value of $4,600. I would have collected over that thirty-six-year period a total of $8,640 in dividends for a total return of $12,590 on my $650 investment, or 1,930 percent. Not bad for the most mature company in the land.

But this is not the end of the story. That $8,640 in dividends would have been paid to me on a quarterly basis over that thirty-six years. If I had opened a savings account in a bank and simply had the dividends sent directly to the savings account, the bank, at the rates that prevailed over that period, would have paid me an additional $7,460 in interest on those dividends. And some of the rates were very low. The Harris Bank paid 1.25 percent on savings accounts for 1946 to 1951, 1.5 percent to 1956, 2 percent to 1959, 3 percent to 1962, 3.5 percent to 1965, 4 percent to 1970, 4.5 percent to 1973, and 5 percent since. These interest payments on the dividends would have brought my total return to $20,050 on a mere $650 investment—a 3,100 percent return. This year, the dividends on the seventy-eight shares plus the interest at 5 percent on the accumulated dividends would amount to $1,001 or a 156 percent return on my original investment.

See what I mean by getting rich from your investments? We have lots of holdings in trust accounts at the Harris with costs as low as $650 and current values of $4,600 or more.

But I didn't hold on to the GM stock. In May 1947 I was living in Chicago and wanted to go to Fort Scott, Kansas, to marry my present wife. I needed money, but I knew no one in Chicago who would cash a check for me. I discovered that the quickest way to get $700 to buy a ring and finance my wedding was to sell my stock. So I did. Now everytime I get irritated with my wife, I silently think to myself, "Three thousand one hundred percent return on my investment." Fortunately, I made a number of other purchases later that I did hold on to. In fact, there have been few years since 1946 that I haven't bought some additional stocks.

The point of this example is, of course, that you do not have to have a lot of money to get started with investments in common stocks, and you do not have to pick some obscure stock to obtain completely satisfactory investment results. Naturally, the more money you have and the greater your talents for picking the right stocks, the better you will do in building your fortune through the ownership of stocks. I would also emphasize that the earlier in life you get started buying stocks, even in small amounts, the more likely you are to end up rich.

Optimism

Well, what else do you need besides money to be a successful investor in common stocks? You need to be an optimist. You need to believe that the free enterprise system will survive and that the future of the United States is bright. If you think our world is going down the drain, you are not going to be able to tolerate the downs of the stock market. Stocks go down as well as up, and when they are down, you should be buying, not beating yourself on the chest and screaming that stocks are confirming your worst suspicions.

If you are not a persistent optimist, you are likely to become discouraged at the wrong time and end up doing the opposite of what you should be doing. I see this over and over in my work at the Harris Bank. We have a whole string of customers who invariably panic and want to get out of the market at the bottom. Then, when the rise comes, the higher the market goes, the greater their enthusiasm. These are people who made their fortune some way other than in the stock market.

Good Judgment

You need good judgment to be a successful stockholder. Some people apparently are born with it. Maybe all people with good judgment are born with it for all I know. Of the people I deal with, some obviously exercise good judgment in everything they do; others consistently display bad judgment. If you have poor judgment in the conduct of your routine affairs, the chances are that you will usually be doing the wrong thing in the stock market. E bonds or savings accounts are probably your best bet.

Good Luck

Any time you have a choice between good luck and good judgment, you should take good luck. Good luck, by definition, denotes success. Good judgment can still go wrong. I have heard of so many people who made good money in stocks through pure good luck, or perhaps you would call it dumb luck.

Several years ago a Presbyterian minister came to see me about his investments. He had been concerned about retirement and had started buying stocks with the idea of supplementing his pension when the time came. His largest holding when I met him was Studebaker, which he had purchased at $6 per share. It was then selling for $18. But I was knowledgeable about Studebaker and knew the company was still in financial difficulty. I knew that Studebaker had been unable to pay its bank loans and that the banks had accepted convertible preferred stock in the company in place of the loans. When bankers are willing to do that, you can bet the company is in desperate circumstances. Yet the stock had gone up from 6 to 18.

So I asked the minister why he had selected Studebaker for his largest purchase. "Well," he said, "Studebaker is a good old name. It has been around a long time, and it seemed cheap at $6 a share." If he had had any idea how bad things were at Studebaker, he would not have touched the stock, but here he had tripled his money. Soon after he had bought the stock, Studebaker came out with its Lark, which enjoyed phenomenal popularity and for a while looked like it was going to save the com-

41

pany. Pure dumb luck. I urged him to sell and take his profits, which he did. The stock then went on up to the mid 30s before completely collapsing. But the minister tripled his money by not knowing anything about what was going on at Studebaker.

One other dumb luck story. Soon after President Kennedy was elected in 1960, a gentleman I heard about, got inside information that Walter Heller was going to be appointed the new president's chairman of the Council of Economic Advisors. So he rushed to his broker and said, "Don't ask me any questions. Just buy me two-hundred shares of Walter Heller Corp." The stock was selling in the mid 40s at the time.

What this gentleman did not know was that the new chairman of the Council of Economic Advisors was an economics professor at the University of Minnesota and had nothing whatsoever to do with the Walter Heller Corp. So he bought the stock for entirely the wrong reason. As it happened, the company's earnings were extremely high at the time and the stock moved up sharply to the mid 90s. At that point, the purchaser discovered that the Heller corporation and the economic advisor with the same name were in no way related, so he rushed back to his broker and ordered him to sell the stock immediately in the mid 90s. Right after he discovered his mistake and sold, the famous Billie Sol Estes scandal broke in Texas, and the Heller company was one of the major losers in this fraud case. So the stock collapsed.

This gentleman was not only lucky once, but twice, and he doubled his money in the process.

Patience

Some of the most successful common stock investors I know are also the most patient people I know. The stock investor who has to make it quick usually experiences a catastrophe. I have a friend who is over ninety years old and is still "trying to make a killing in Wall Street." These are his words. He is comfortably fixed, but not wealthy. He tells me that if he had just held on to the Union Carbide stock he bought in 1916 he would be more than a millionaire now. So his churning around, worrying about every one-eights decline, and trying to hit it big quickly have kept him from making it big.

I have another friend who is just the opposite. He is in his seventies, worth several million. He buys stocks that are down and out and are selling at big discounts from asset values, and then he exercises extreme patience. He says that he is in no hurry, that he has plenty of time. He just wants to be holding the stock when something good happens to all those assets to make them more valuable. He had a real heyday during the conglomerate period of the late 1960s. That is when Gulf & Western, ITT, and other conglomerates were gobbling up all kinds of distressed stocks that were selling at a fraction of their asset values. They took a lot of my patient friend's stocks at two, three, and even four times what he had paid for them, many of which he had bought years before. He was indeed holding them when something happened to make them more valuable.

Courage

A very important ingredient of successful stock investing is courage. The courage to buy when others are selling; the courage to buy when stocks are hitting new lows; the courage to buy when the economy looks bad; courage to buy at the bottom. If you look back over the years, you will note that the times when the gloom was the thickest invariably turned out to have been the best times to buy stocks.

But most people like to buy when everything is rosy and stocks are hitting new highs. That takes no courage. There is a great tendency to think that stocks will continue doing whatever it is they have been doing. If they have been going up, they will continue going up forever, think the masses. If they are hitting new lows, they will continue hitting new lows forever. Maybe they will continue declining a while longer after you buy them, but you are not likely to be able to know when the bottom has been reached. So your best bet is to pick a level you are willing to pay and proceed with part of your investment funds. If they go lower,

43

you can buy more at even better prices. If they turn and go up, then you will make a profit on what you have.

When To Buy Common Stocks

Now, regardless of when now is, is always the hardest time to know with any degree of certainty whether it is a good time to buy common stocks. With the benefit of good old hindsight, it is always easy to look back and identify times when it was a good or bad time to buy stocks. But the investor is always faced with what to do now. You simply do not have hindsight available to you at the time you make your purchase.

On January 2, 1976, we gave the subscribers to one of the investment services provided by the Harris Bank a list of twelve stocks that we thought were attractive for purchase at the time. The stock market seemed to be in a rising phase at the time and did in fact continue up rather sharply, these twelve stocks along with it. In April 1976, a nonsubscriber who had seen our January 2 suggestions wrote to us, saying, "Of course, it was easy to pick stocks in January that would go up. What do you suggest now?" I had news for this lady. It was not any easier on January 2, 1976, to pick stocks that might go up than it was at the time she wrote in April 1976. The hindsight that was available to her in April simply made it look easier.

Granted that now is always the tough time to determine whether stocks should be bought, there are some times when you can act with a higher degree of confidence than at other times, and I can identify a few such times.

Recessions

That you don't buy stocks when business is bad and getting worse is a very popular misconception. I hear it over and over every time we get into a recession, and so I went and looked at how stock prices acted in every recession we have had since 1910.

Table 1

Recession started	Stocks bottomed and started rising	Recession ended	Approximate number of months stocks rose before end of recession
Jan. 1910	9/25/11	Jan. 1912	4
Jan. 1913	*	Dec. 1914	*
Aug. 1918	2/ 8/19	Apr. 1919	3
Jan. 1920	8/24/21	July 1921	(1)
May 1923	8/27/23	July 1924	11
Oct. 1926	10/19/26**	Nov. 1927	12**
June 1929	7/ 8/32	Mar. 1933	9
May 1937	3/31/38	June 1938	3
Feb. 1945	3/16/45	Oct. 1945	8
Nov. 1948	6/13/49	Oct. 1949	4
July 1953	9/14/53	Aug. 1954	11
July 1957	10/22/57	Apr. 1958	6
May 1960	10/25/60	Feb. 1961	4
Sept. 1969	5/26/70	Nov. 1970	6
Nov. 1973	12/ 6/74	Apr. 1975	5
Jan. 1980	3/27/80	July 1980	4
July 1981	8/11/82	Dec. 1982	4

Average 5.6 months

* The New York Stock Exchange was closed from 7/13/14 to 12/12/14 because of the outbreak of World War I. It was at a four-year low of 71.42 on the old twelve-stock average when it closed on 7/12/14. It opened on 12/12/14 at 74.56 and moved up from there for several years.

** Stock prices moved up right through the 1926 recession.

You will note from Table 1 that the recession that started in January 1910 continued through January 1912. The Dow Jones industrial average, which then consisted of twelve stocks, bottomed out and started up on September 25, 1911, about four months before the end of the recession. This is its usual pattern. In twelve of the fifteen recessions we have had since 1910 stocks turned up three to eleven months before the end of the recession. The average length of the upturn before each of these twelve recessions ended was 5.6 months. The market actions in 1914 cannot be determined because the Exchange was closed for five months. In 1921 stocks reached their low about a month after the end of the recession. This was the only time in the fifteen recessions that the economy turned up before stocks did. In 1926 stocks had been in a general rising trend for several years and just continued rising right through that recession.

In spite of these few obscurities, the pattern is clearly established that stock prices rise well ahead of the business recovery. Thus, what you really need to know is when you are within about 5.6 months of the bottom of the recession. If you wait until business has clearly picked up before buying stocks, you will miss the initial rise, and that is usually the most rewarding part of the rise.

Perhaps it would be interesting to see how much the market rises from its low to the end of the recession. Table 2 shows this.

In past recessions, if you had waited until the last day of the recession to buy your stocks, you would have missed rises of 10 to 42 percent from the market lows. There is, however, no

Table 2

Stock market low	Recession ended	Percent gain in stocks from market low to end of recession	Percent gain in stocks from market low to three months after end of recession
9/25/11	Jan. 1912	10%	24%
*See note above	Dec. 1914	—	—
2/ 8/19	Apr. 1919	16	38
8/24/21	July 1921	—	13
8/27/23	July 1924	19	21
10/19/26	Nov. 1927	36	33
7/ 8/32	Mar. 1933	34	138
3/31/38	June 1938	35	43
3/16/45	Oct. 1945	23	34
6/13/49	Oct. 1949	17	25
9/14/53	Aug. 1954	31	51
10/22/57	Apr. 1958	10	20
10/25/60	Feb. 1961	17	25
5/26/70	Nov. 1970	26	39
12/ 6/74	Apr. 1975	42	44
3/27/80	July 1980	23	22
8/11/82	Dec. 1982	38	41

way to know when the last day of the recession has arrived. In fact, it is invariably two or three months after the recession has ended that we can look back and, with hindsight, identify approximately when it ended.

How much of the rise from the bottom would you have missed in these past recessions if you had recognized three months later that the recession was over and only then concluded that the time was right to buy the Dow Jones industrial average? The last column on the right shows that you would have missed a rise of between 13 to 138 percent from the bottom of the market.

Discouraging, isn't it? You would think that the market would be logical enough to wait until after it becomes clear to all of us that the recession is over and the economy is improving before it proceeds to go up. But the market obviously follows a different type of logic. The stock market is a phenomenal anticipator of future events, both good and bad. That is the reason it invariably goes up before a recession ends and down before a recession starts.

Beginning of Economic Recovery

Suppose you are not one to take the risk of buying stocks when business is bad and getting worse. In the interest of minimizing your market risk, you are willing to forego the early rise that takes place before the recession is over. How much time do you usually have from the beginning of the economic recovery to still make money in the market? Table 2 showed the percentage changes in the market from the bottom of the market to the end of the recession and from the bottom of the market to three months after the end of the recession. Table 3 indicates the time available to act after the end of the recession. In thirteen of the economic recoveries we have had since 1912, the market continued going up for an average of 18.3 months after the end of the recession and the beginning of the recovery. In one of the recoveries, the one starting in November 1927, the market went up right through the recession, and that recovery is not included in the 18.3-month average.

47

Date Recession Ended	Table 3 Date Market Topped*	Approximate Months Rise
Jan. 1912	9/30/12	8
Dec. 1914	12/ 2/16	24
Apr. 1919	11/ 3/19	6
July 1921	3/20/23	20
July 1924	9/ 3/29	61
Nov. 1927	**	—
Mar. 1933	2/ 5/34	8
June 1938	11/12/38	5
Oct. 1945	5/29/46	7
Oct. 1949	1/ 5/53	38
Aug. 1954	8/ 2/56	24
Apr. 1958	1/ 5/60	20
Feb. 1961	3/15/62	13
Nov. 1970	1/11/73	25
Apr. 1975	9/22/76	16
July 1980	4/27/81	9
Dec. 1982	??	??

Average 18.3 Months

* Dow Jones Industrial Average
** Market went up right through this recession.

The rises have varied from a low of five months in 1938 to a whopping sixty-one-month rise following the 1924 recession. If we omit the abnormal sixty-one-month rise, we get an average of 14.8 months for the remaining fourteen periods of rising markets.

Of course, the market did not go straight up during all those months. There were numerous periods of no progress and even of irregular declines, which at the time doubtless seemed an eternity to the impatient investor. But if you have good economic insight and can determine with conviction when the recession ended, history shows that you have several months—an average of 18.3 months since 1910—in which to buy stocks with a high degree of confidence. You will make money if your stock selections perform reasonably close to the Dow Jones averages.

In Table 3 we are talking about the periods of time during which the market continued up after the end of the recession.

Now let's see, in Table 4, how much the market went up after each recession before it entered a sustained down trend.

Table 4
DOW JONES INDUSTRIAL AVERAGE

Date Recession Ended	High for Month Recession Ended	Subsequent High Attained Before Sustained Down Turn	Percent Rises
Jan. 1912	82.36	94.13	14.2%
Dec. 1914	56.76	106.81	88.0
Apr. 1919	93.51	119.62	28.0
July 1921	69.86	105.38	49.5
July 1924	102.14	381.17	270.0
Nov. 1927	198.21	—	—
Mar. 1933	62.95	110.74	76.0
June 1938	135.87	158.41	16.7
Oct. 1945	187.06	212.50	13.2
Oct. 1949	190.36	293.79	54.0
Aug. 1954	350.38	520.95	49.0
Apr. 1958	455.86	685.47	50.0
Feb. 1961	662.08	723.54	9.3
Nov. 1970	794.09	1,051.70	32.5
Apr. 1975	858.13	1,026.30	20.0
July 1980	936.18	1,024.05	9.4
Dec. 1982	1070.55	??	??

Average 50.9%

Some of the percentage rises following the end of the recession were not much, such as the 9.3 percent gain after the 1961 recession. Most were very extensive. The average rise following 13 recessions, including the abnormal 1924–1929 rise, was 57.8 percent. Excluding the 1924–1929 rise, the average gain was 40.1 percent.

So we repeat, if your economic insight is good enough that you can determine with conviction when a recession is over, you can hardly miss making money in the stock market. At least, that is the way it has been in the past.

Bottom of The Market Low

The hardest time to make up your mind to buy stocks is when they are going down. You always think that maybe you can buy your choice stock cheaper tomorrow. And that is right so long as the market keeps going down. But the market does eventually hit bottom and start going up. At least it always has in the past. If you just had that ultimate of foresight and could know when the market is at the bottom, you would have it made.

Suppose you do have good enough hindsight to look back and recognize that the market bottomed out a month or two months or six months or even a year ago. Does this mean you have missed out completely or is there probably still time for you to participate in a further rise? Table 5 shows how the market has acted following each sharp decline since World War II.

Table 5
STOCK MARKET RECOVERIES AFTER LOWS

Dow Jones Industrial Average		Percent	Percent	Percent
Date Hit Bottom	Close	Percent Down From Previous High	Change during next six months	Change during second six months	Change during third six months
6 /13/49	161.60	−24%	+22%	+18%	+ 2%
9/14/53	255.49	−13	+17	+20	+16
10/22/57	419.79	−19	+ 7	+22	+20
10/25/60	566.05	−17	+17	+ 7	− 3
6/26/62	535.76	−27	+22	+10	+ 8
10/7/66	744.32	−26	+27	− 2	− 9
5/26/70	631.16	−36	+23	+20	+19
12/6/74	577.60	−45	+45	− 3	+25
2/28/78	742.12	−28	+18	− 8	+10
8/11/82	777.21	−24	+40	+8	−2

Suppose on June 13, 1949, you had concluded that the market had gone down long enough and far enough. The market at that time had been in a downward trend ever since May 31, 1946. By June 13, 1949, it was down a discouraging 24 percent, and by that time hoards of investors had lost interest in the stock market. But June 13, 1949, was a big turning point. Over the next six months it picked up almost all of that long three-year loss with a 22 percent gain. Thus, you had to be insightful and decisive to get in on the best part of the rise. Imagine going up as much in six months as it had gone down in three years!

But suppose you missed the first six months of the rise? Is it too late for you to participate? Not usually. In the 1949 rise it went up another beautiful 18 percent in the second six-month period and an additional 2 percent in the third six-month period. And this is not an unusual pattern as shown by the Table 5. The rise following the October 7, 1966, bottom was the notable exception. In that market move, if you missed the first six-month rise, you missed the whole thing. It was a long wait before you participated in any gain.

The bigger the drop, the faster the rise tends to be. The 1974 decline of 45 percent was the sharpest in the postwar period. It was followed by the sharpest six-month rise in the post war period (45 percent), and if you missed the first six-month rise you had to wait patiently for several months to get in on the subsequent rise as the market actually declined 3 percent in the second six-month period before rising another 25 percent in the third six-month period.

Table 5 does not show it, but there tends to be a further good rise in the fourth six-month period. Actually, the pattern for the fourth six-month period is better than for the third six months. Apparently investors tend to decide late in the second six-month period and early in the third six months that the rise has gone far enough, so they sell to take profits. Then, in the fourth six-month period, they decide to come back in, and this creates a good performance in most of the fourth six-month periods.

But watch out for the fifth and sixth six-month periods. Those are hard times to make money in the market with any degree of consistency. In the fifth six-month periods since World War II, we have had three significantly up markets, three significantly down markets, and two markets essentially unchanged, which means your odds for a significant gain or a significant loss were about fifty-fifty. I like better odds than that. In the sixth six-

51

month period, we had one significantly up market, three significantly down markets, and three essentially unchanged. The odds are strongly against you in those periods.

The easy conclusion to be drawn from the market actions since World War II is that even if you miss the big rise in the first six months after the market turns up, you can still have a fairly high degree of confidence there is more rise to come. However, the further you get away from the bottom of the market, the more the odds start building against you.

Even if you can figure out where you are in the market swings, there is always an inclination to think that this time is different. I hear this over and over in both down and up markets. And I will readily admit there are always a few obvious differences in the circumstances that are influencing the market, but I would submit that the differences are seldom significant. Just look at the persistence of the pattern in the market actions shown in Table 5. History does repeat itself in the investment areas as well as in other areas, and maybe even more so in investments.

Elections—Democrats or Republicans

Suppose your favorite presidential candidate wins. Is this in itself reason for you to become optimistic about stock prices? Or take the reverse of this. Suppose your candidate loses? Should you sell your stocks? Is one of the parties good for stocks and one bad? If so, which party?

Most investors are Republicans. How do I know? Look what happened to stock prices immediately after President Carter's election on November 2, 1976. It went down 4.4 percent in the next seven trading days. This is at a catastrophic annual rate of minus 200 percent which, of course, is impossible to sustain.

But this is what usually happens when Democrats get elected. Going back forty-four years to President Roosevelt in 1932, from the day before the election in November 1932 to the end of the month, the market dropped a whopping 13 percent—this despite the fact that the market had already collapsed! This proved the accuracy of a short poem I have heard many times and cannot resist quoting here.

> From the day you are born
> To the day you rent a hearse
> Things are never so bad
> That they can't get worse.

I am not sure this poem has an author or at least an author who will admit that he is the author.

When Mr. Truman was elected in November 1948, the market dropped 10 percent by the end of the month. When Mr. Kennedy was elected in 1960, the market ended the month almost exactly where it closed the day before the election.

But look what happens when Republicans get elected. Here again we are taking the Dow Jones Industrial close the day before the election to the end of November.

> Hoover (1928)—up 15 percent
> Eisenhower (1952)—up 5 percent
> Nixon (1968)—up 4 percent
> Reagan (1980)—up 6 percent

So, including Mr. Carter, the market immediately went down sharply three out of four times when Democrats got elected and immediately went up sharply four out of four times when Republicans got elected. This proves that Democrats arc bad and Republicans are good for stock prices, doesn't it? Before agreeing with this conclusion, let's see how stocks acted during the term or terms of each.

> Roosevelt—up 165 percent
> Truman—up 71 percent
> Kennedy/Johnson—up 60 percent
> Carter—down 3 percent

From the day before the election in November 1932 to the day before Mr. Roosevelt died (April 11, 1945), the market went up

53

165 percent. Sure that was a long period of more than twelve years with a lot of ups and downs, but even so, a 165 percent rise was pretty good. And this figure doesn't include dividends.

From the day before Mr. Truman's surprise election in November 1948 until the day before the 1952 election, a mere four years, the market went up a big 71 percent. And this single term covered a recession and a war.

During the Kennedy/Johnson eight-year period the market went up 60 percent, not including dividends paid. Mr. Carter was the one Democrat exception. The market ended his term almost exactly where it had started. Now for the Republicans:

> Hoover—down 78 percent
> Eisenhower—up 120 percent
> Nixon/Ford—up 2 percent

The Dow Jones average closed the day before the 1976 election only 2 percent above where it closed the day before Mr. Nixon's election in 1968. Not much progress for an eight year period. It frequently fluctuates this much in a month's or even a week's time.

So during the four periods of Democratic rule, we had three big winners in the market. During the three Republican periods, we had one big loser, one big winner, and one draw.

Were these stock movements just a series of coincindences with no historical relevance? Is this a useless exercise in trying to determine how stocks may fare under a Democratic or Republican administration? I don't think so. I think stocks always reflect investors' collective expectations for future earnings and dividends. If it appears that Democrat or Republican policies are good for corporate profits, then we are likely to have an up market. If their policies appear to be bad for profits, we have a down market.

Every four years at election time we hear over and over that the Republicans create recessions and unemployment and that the Democrats create inflation. History over the past forty-eight years seems to support both of these allegations. In Mr. Hoover's term we had severe deflation and high unemployment. The Federal Reserve System reduced the money supply by more than 30 percent. Any time the Federal Reserve reduces the money supply by this magnitude we will have a depression. And it did happen under a Republican administration. Mr. Roosevelt initiated extensive programs to stimulate the economy, primarily by massive Federal deficit spending. By the end of the Roosevelt/Truman period we had had prolonged inflation. Of course two wars came in there, and inflation invariably accompanies wars, but we see no point in blaming the wars on the Democrats in this discussion. We are talking here about inflations and recessions.

When Mr. Eisenhower took office in early 1953, he was preoccupied with inflation because we had had a lot of it over the preceding twenty years and the American people were concerned about it. We had three recessions during Mr. Eisenhower's eight years in office, which the Harris's economist, Dr. Beryl W. Sprinkel, says would be hard to accomplish even if you tried, but Mr. Eisenhower stopped the inflation. From 1954 through mid 1965 we had inflation of only about 1.3% per year. Unemployment was fairly high, and the lack of economic growth was an issue in the 1960 elections, but inflation had been eliminated as a national concern.

Mr. Eisenhower so completely wrung the inflation out of the economy that it took four and one-half years of stimulative policies initiated by the Kennedy/Johnson administration to get it going again. It wasn't until mid 1965 that unemployment got down and inflation took off again. During the eight-year Kennedy/Johnson period, inflation rose from 1.3 percent per year to around 6 percent.

Mr. Nixon made reducing inflation his first order of business when he took office in early 1969 and he succeeded beautifully initially. He had a recession in 1970, but for the month of July 1971 the Cost of Living Index was up a mere 3.8 percent compared to 6 percent when he assumed the presidency less than two years before. In August 1971 Mr. Nixon made the biggest mistake that has been made in the management of our economy since

55

the Federal Reserve reduced the money supply so drastically during the Hoover administration. He put on wage-price controls. This simply hived up a good part of the inflation that was in the economy and released it in 1974 when the controls were removed. But even with the frightening double-digit inflation of 1974, by the time Mr. Ford lost the election in November 1976, the inflation rate was under 4 percent which was materially lower than when Mr. Nixon took over. Mr. Carter took us to 16 percent.

So we do have a long history in which the Democrats have openly and aggressively sought to stimulate economic growth. During these periods corporate profits and stock prices have tended to do well, and inflation has followed. Either by historical rhythm or by design the Republicans have found themselves in a position of required economic restraint to get inflation down. And this restraint, except during Eisenhower's term, tended to be bad for stock prices. What would happen to stock prices, inflation, and corporate profits if either Democrats or Republicans stayed in control forever? We do not know. We are only examining the past here in the hopes it will help us in our investments in the future. And for the past fifty-two years or so, stocks have tended to do better under the Democrats than under the Republicans.

As an investor, your goal is to take advantage of the situation you find yourself in, and this may not always be to your political liking at all. It is all right to try to change things you don't like, but it is foolhardy to destroy yourself or your investment career just because the party not of your choice wins the election. I should know; I have voted for few winners since I switched parties thirty years ago.

Should You Buy and Hold or Buy and Sell?

The answer to this question depends on three things:

1. The type of stock market you are in
2. The type of stocks you are buying
3. The type of person you are

I started buying stocks for my personal account in October 1946. In the late 1940s I adopted a policy of selling any time a $500 gain was available ($500 was a lot of money for me back then). This policy worked great through mid 1953. This was a period when the market itself was going nowhere except for modest fluctuations up and down.

In mid 1953 this all changed. The market still fluctuated up and down but mostly up. In 1956 it dawned on me that all of the sales I had made since 1953 had been big mistakes. For example, I bought an odd lot of Goodyear in 1951 at 40. It went to 60, back down to 38, up to 62, and back to 40. At that point I made a firm decision, namely, if this thing goes back to 60 again someone else can have it. It went back to 60, and some lucky buyer took it. It then went to 109 and split two for one. The split stock went to 154 and split three for one.

The same type of thing happened to National Lead (now NL Industries). I bought it at 29 in 1953 and was elated to sell at 42. It then rushed up to 138 and split three for one.

Why the selling mistakes? Because the whole market changed in mid 1953 from a moderately fluctuating market to a strong up market. This strong upward market lasted until early 1966. The Dow Jones industrial average went from 254 in mid 1953 to 1001 in early 1966. Sure, there were some down markets during that period, but each down market stopped well above the prior down market, thus sustaining a long upward trend. Any good stock (and most weak ones) bought and held during that thirteen-year period did well. Almost any stock sold during that period was a mistake.

Then why didn't I change from a buy-and-sell policy to a buy-and-hold policy in mid 1953 before making those big mistakes with Goodyear and National Lead? Because it invariably takes two or three years for most investors to recognize, or at least become convinced, that a real change in the market has taken place. Thus the costly mistakes tend to be made in the early phase of the changed market, before the investor realizes that the nature of the market has changed.

From early 1966 through mid 1982 the market went nowhere except violently up and down. During this period a policy of buy and sell would have been a productive exercise, whereas buy and hold produced nothing but repeated frustrations.

Of course you need the right rhythm to make out well on a buy-and-sell policy during periods like that. You have to buy when the market is down and sell when it is up. If you get caught up in the rhythm of buying at the peak and selling at the bottom, your career as an investor will be short.

It looks simple doesn't it? Just buy when the market is down and sell when it is up and get rich fast. To recap briefly, this practice would have been very good from mid 1946 to mid 1953 but very bad from mid 1953 to early 1966, then very good again from early 1966 at least through mid 1982.

The second consideration is what type of stocks you are buying. Are they growth stocks, highly cyclical stocks, or income producing stocks? This has a lot of do with whether you should be buying and holding or buying and selling.

IBM is the premier growth stock of our generation. It is the ideal type of stock for the buyers and holders. Its earnings have been in an orderly rising trend since about 1916. So long as earnings keep rising, the price of the stock will eventually follow. Even if you pay too high a price for the stock, the rising earnings will ultimately bail you out. This has happened repeatedly to IBM stockholders. Investors periodically run the price up too high, and this is followed by a sell-off that gets it back in better relationship with other investment alternatives. But any sales of IBM stock between 1916 and 1983 would have been better had they not been made.

I am not saying that IBM should never be sold. Obviously, it cannot go on forever increasing its earnings 12 percent or more per year. The time will come when this will change, but I do not anticipate that change any time in the foreseeable future. What I am saying here is that if you are a buyer and seller, you are likely to avoid more gains by selling IBM than by holding it. If you are a buyer and holder, this is an ideal stock for you to buy. Look what it did during the long period of no progress by the Dow Jones averages from early 1966 through 1976. In early 1966 when the Dow Jones average reached 1001, IBM was selling at 138. By the end of 1976 when the Dow got back to 1000 again, IBM was up to 270. Its earnings in 1966 were $3.77 per share compared to $15.94 in 1976.

Other good stocks that have served buyers and holders well in the past are American Home Products, Beatrice Foods, Baxter Laboratories (now Baxter-Travenol), Bristol-Myers, Merck, and Abbott Laboratories. These companies increased their earnings year after year, and the price of their stocks went up beautifully even over that long period of no real progress by the Dow Jones averages.

Your success in buying and holding depends on your ability to pick stocks that will continue increasing their earnings. You invariably have to pay a premium price for a growth type stock, and if it stops growing after you buy it, you are just as invariably in for a disappointing adjustment. An excellent example of this is the Western Publishing Company stock. This company increased its sales and earnings for something like fifty three years then went public in 1960 at 42. Then it reported moderately down earnings for two years straight, and the stock quickly adjusted from selling like a growth stock to one with moderate growth and income at around 18 where it remained for years. With a few down years it simply lost its image as a growth stock. This is the sort of thing buyers and holders of growth stocks need to avoid. How do you avoid this? That is the tough assignment. That is what investments are all about. That is what keeps us all from getting rich quickly and easily.

What about stocks for buying and selling? Here you need to use stocks that characteristically go up and down sharply over the shortest periods of time available. You should use stocks that respond drastically to changes in the economy. Typical stocks of this type are the autos, metals, airlines, most chemicals, papers, truckers, machinery, building, and so on. Look at General Motors stock during the period when the market was going from

1001 in early 1966 to 980 in late 1976. General Motors was selling at 105 in early 1966. By late 1966 it had dropped to 68. It recovered to 79 in late 1968, dropped to 58 in mid 1970, up to 90 in mid 1971, down to 28 in late 1974, and back to 78 in late 1976. This is a good solid company, but its stock goes up and down like a roller coaster, frequently ending where it started just like a roller coaster. If you really want to play the wide swings in the market, look at Chrysler's market action during this period. The weaker stocks in each cyclical industry tend to drop the most in a weak economy and rise the most in a strong economy. Thus, if you are good at determining the economic trends and are by nature a buyer and seller, the best opportunities are in the weaker stocks of the cyclical industries. One word of warning, however: you better avoid those that are so weak they may not survive.

But here again you have to have the rhythm of buying low and selling high. Don't get caught up in the enthusiasm when all looks great and give up in despair when things look bad. That too will cut your investment career short.

Now for the third factor in determining whether it is better to buy and hold or buy and sell. What kind of a person are you in terms of your investment approach? Do you enjoy taking gains even though it means paying a tax? Do you feel that you (or your investment advisor) are not working hard enough unless frequent trades are being made? Are you gifted in picking stocks that are about to go up? Do you have the courage to buy them when they are down and out (like 1974) and sell them when everything looks rosy? If you can answer all of these questions "yes," then you are probably a successful buyer and seller of stocks.

On the other hand, if you hate paying taxes, or dislike frequent changes, or tend to take pride of ownership in the business when you buy stock in it, or like to know just how much in dividends you will be getting each quarter, you are probaly a buyer and holder.

Fortunately you don't have to be one to the complete exclusion of the other. Most of the investors I know who tend to consider themselves buyers and sellers also have some stock holdings that they do not want disturbed for a variety of reasons. The stocks they want held are invariably ones that have gone up and frequently involve some kind of family or business connections. We seldom find an investor who is a pure buyer and seller with no allegiance or sentimental attachment to any of his stocks.

Should You Buy Stocks For Capital Appreciation or For Current Income?

The answer to this question depends on two things:

1. How old you are
2. How much money you have

Suppose, for example, you are thirty years old and have a well-paying job, as most thirty-year-olds do these days. Suppose you do not have any accumulated assets to speak of as most thirty-year-olds do not have these days. But you want to better your situation as life continues to treat you well.

Clearly you should be buying growth stocks, that is, stocks whose past records has been one of persistent growth in earnings and whose future prospects for continued growth seem good. Stated another way, you should look for stocks that can reasonably be expected to attain capital appreciation over a period of time as the increased earnings are reflected in the price of the stock. A "period of time" is important here because a thirty-year-old investor has plenty of time.

A thirty-year-old investor of this type may even engage in some pure venture capital investments if he is of this temperament. Remember, under our assumptions, he has little or nothing now except his good salary, and he will never have much unless his investments pay off well for him. So what if he makes a mistake that loses most or all of his investment? He has thirty-five years of gainful employment ahead of him in which to make

61

it up. An aggressive, high-risk approach is not out of order for an investor of this type.

Now change this example just a little. Suppose this thirty-year-old inherits $1 million. Does this mean he is now in a position to take big risks? Not at all. Not with his whole $1 million. Remember, he did not earn or make the $1 million himself. He inherited it, so he has not yet proved himself a successful risk-taker. It would be foolish of him to put all his $1 million inheritance in high-risk investments of any kind. The difference between $1 million and $2 million is not that great, but the difference between $1 million and nothing is catastrophic.

So a thirty-year-old with an inherited $1 million should put a certain proportion, say 40 to 50 percent, in high-grade, fixed income securities as storm-cellar protection against ever being poor again. He or she will still have plenty of money for risk taking for a person of limited experience.

Now suppose the investor is sixty or more years old and is faced with mandatory retirement at age sixty-five. Regardless of how much or how little he has, it is now time to lean heavily toward safety of principal. Of course he need not fold up his tent and withdraw from the investment world just because he has reached age sixty, but time has essentially run out for taking high risks. If he loses his assets at this stage in life he does not have all of those years of gainful employment ahead of him in which to recoup his losses. He can be faced with a subsistence level retirement, and that can be tragic.

Does this mean all bonds by age sixty, seventy, or eighty? Not necessarily. But it certainly does mean some bonds. It usually means a comfortable balance between stocks and bonds, depending on the amount of assets available and the income and safety needs of the investor. As you well know, bonds provide both the highest income and the greatest degree of safety today. That has not always been the case. Prior to 1956 stocks yielded more than bonds, but not any more. Thus, the greater the investor's need for maximum income, the higher the proportion of his investments should be in bonds. Also, the greater the need for safety of principal, the higher the proportion in bonds. Sometimes the need for maximum income and the greatest degree of safety of principal does exist to such an extent that the investments should be in bonds only.

One of the major problems in determining suitable investments for older people is the difficulty of trying to estimate how long they might live. The actuarial tables are quite good for large groups, but can be very misleading when applied to one individual. We had a dramatic example of this at the Harris Bank many years ago. A trust account was set up for a nice lady who was eighty years old at the time. The bank invested one hundred percent of the money in bonds "because of the advanced age of the beneficiary." She then lived to be the oldest person in the State of Illinois and died at age 111. The remaindermen raised some embarrassing questions about the management of the funds as this turned out to be a prolonged period of rising stock prices. The account would have fared much better if we had been less concerned about her "advanced age." Nevertheless, reduced risk-taking is invariably in order as the investor reaches or passes retirement age.

What about investors between age thirty and sixty? This gets too detailed for discussion here except to say that in all cases, regardless of how old or how young you are, how much or how little money you have, your investments must be selected so as to reasonably be expected to do for you what you want done otherwise you will have repeated frustrations.

I once knew a school teacher who bought for income only. He looked upon his stocks as a purchase of income, not an investment in common stocks. He considered each purchase as a salary increase. Each time he bought a stock he would announce to his close friends something like this, "I got a $200 a year raise today." The friends would invariably say, "How come?" because other school teachers were not getting raises at that time. His answer would be, "I bought one hundred shares of XYZ stock, and it pays a $2 dividend." The more stocks he bought, the higher his income rose, and the higher his income rose, the more stocks he bought.

When this gentleman died, the newspapers were trying to figure out how he ever accumulated such a large estate on his modest salary. This was back in the days when school teachers were not well paid. He spent no time whining about his low salary or the inadequacy of his wage increases. He simply arranged his own increases by buying dividend-paying stocks.

For this investor, income was his sole consideration. His stocks did appreciate, but that was not his goal. He may well have accumulated more wealth over those years by buying growth type stocks, but that was clearly not his approach and probably would not have worked well for him. To have forced him into the growth cult would probably have been a big mistake. He had an investment approach that he understood and liked, and it served him well. He lived a very happy life and died a wealthy and respected man.

In buying common stocks, you should look at your own personal situation including your age, your risk-taking ability, your ability to tolerate losses as well as gains, your outlook on life, your goals, expectations, and needs, and follow a course with which you can be comfortable at all times. Otherwise you are likely to flit from one approach to another, depending on the investment fads of the time, and end up broke, disillusioned, frustrated, or even bitter at the world.

The United States of America—Still The Land Of Opportunity For All

"You can't get rich in this country anymore because of taxes," says the excuser. Or he might blame inflation, government regulations, union restrictions, competition from big corporations, lack of unexploited areas, or any number of supposed obstacles. On and on it goes, excuses for not succeeding today. To heck you can't get rich anymore. I have no statistics to prove it, but I would guess that more people have become millionaires in the past ten years than in any prior ten-year period in our history. Sure, inflation had a lot to do with it, and for that reason a million dollars today is not worth nearly as much as a million dollars ten years ago, but nevertheless, a million dollars is rich as far as I am concerned. The Internal Revenue Service does report the number of taxpayers each year who have income of $1 million or more, and this number keeps going up. Of course, this is before taxes.

Sure, the rules of the game are changing, but the changes in this country are evolutionary and not revolutionary. The astute investors simply adjust to the changes and, in many cases, use the changes to their advantage. Changes of all kinds invariably create opportunities for some at the same time they produce hardships or catastrophes for others. Look what great opportunities increased government regulation has created for the paper and computer industries.

Our economy is so big, so diverse, and so progressive that it creates phenomenal opportunities for all who want to use their muscle, brains, or money to advance their financial well being. Well, how big is our economy and what does it mean to people who want to get rich?

The Gross National Product (GNP) in 1983 will be about $3,500 billion; this is three trillion, five hundred billion dollars. This is the total value of goods and services produced in the United States in one year.

It is an estimated figure by the Department of Commerce, but we think it is a fairly good estimate despite its various shortcomings. It does not for example, include the value of the services of the 60 million housewives in America, and who would deny that they perform a valuable service? On the other hand, it does include the value of medical services. Thus, the more people get sick and go to the doctor, the greater this segment contributes to the whole. Look what would happen if all 231 million of us got real sick. The GNP would skyrocket, and this would suggest a great business boom, but in reality it would merely be reflecting the fact that we all got sick.

The GNP is a single-figure measure of how well off we are. If the GNP is up in real dollars (excluding inflation), we say we are in a period of prosperity. If the GNP is flat, politicians who are out of office start screaming about economic stagnation. "We must get the economy going again," they say. And we must keep the economy rising because the labor force is rising. New jobs must be created for these new workers otherwise unemployment will rise. If the GNP is down in real terms for two consecutive quarters, we say we are in a recession. So none of us can avoid being affected one way or another by this phenomenal GNP number whether it is up, flat, or declining.

Some highly intelligent people contend that we Americans place too much emphasis on our GNP numbers, on our material well being, that we should be more interested in human rights instead of property rights. Frankly, I am unable to separate property rights from human rights. It seems to me that human rights are property rights, that what the underpriviledged are demanding today is a larger share in the property rights. If we had more goods and services, we could improve the standard of living of more people.

But someone has to produce these goods and services. They do not just appear from nowhere for our enjoyment. Production is the effective use of three things: (1) management, (2) labor, and (3) capital. There are 231 million people in the United States. With a GNP of $3,500 billion, that works out to $15,200 per man, woman, and child in the United States. Thus, if your contribution to the output of goods and services is worth less than $15,200 you are contributing less than the national average. I have a wife and two children, none of whom are doing anything that gets included in the GNP figures, so I must produce goods and services worth $60,800 just to equal the national average as head of a family of four.

What you produce is not the same as your salary. The value of your production must exceed your salary, or else no employer will keep you on the payroll. But don't forget the productivity of your investments in calculating your contribution. Capital is one of the three elements of production and is just as essential to the productive processes as labor and management. Without capital, labor and management would not be needed. Many people, including some political leaders, seem not to realize this, and we will have more to say about this later. The important thing to keep in mind here is that you, as a worker, have an opportunity to participate in our vast economic output in two ways: (1) through your labor, and (2) through the use of your capital. And keep in mind that it is the use of your capital that can make you rich. Your labor is a means of making a living and also of generating some capital for use in making you rich.

The huge size of our economy is what creates opportunities for you to get rich. According to figures prepared by the Department of Commerce, in the International Economic Report of the President, our economy accounts for about 26 percent of the world's output of goods and services. These huge numbers don't mean much until they are related to the number of people involved, and here is the amazing thing about our economy. We only have a little over 6 percent of the world's people in the United States. Thus, we have the unusual phenomenon of 6 percent of the world's population producing and consuming about 26 percent of the world's goods and services. This means the productivity of our labor force is far higher than the average for the rest of the world. In addition, our economy is heavily oriented toward consumer products, whereas other parts of the world that have a high per capita output tend to have an economy based on extractive products.

In terms of the consumer items that are nearest and dearest to most of us, our 6 percent of the world's population has about 44 percent of the world's autos, 36 percent of the world's TV sets, and 42 percent of the world's telephones. We can put every man, woman, and child in the United States in our autos at one time and have an average of 2.1 people in each car. If Russia did this, they would have 45 people in each auto, China 207, and India 594.

We can sit every person in the United States in front of our TV sets at one time and have an average of only 2 people before each set. China would have 1,660. But we can only put 65 percent of our people on the telephone at any one time. The other 35 percent must wait. However, this creates no real problem for us because few people can drive a car, watch TV, and talk on the phone all at one time.

This 6 percent of the world's population consumes 41 percent of the world's aluminum, 25 percent of the world's copper, and 33 percent of the world's total energy supply.

Did you realize we drink an average of 21.1 gallons of beer per man, woman, and child per year? Since a lot of children don't drink any, some grown-ups have to drink a lot. Did you drink your fair share? If you live in Wisconsin, you probably did since there they drink an average of 30 gallons per man, woman, and child. If you live in Alabama you probably did not since they drink only 13.9 gallons. They are big Coca-Cola drinkers down there.

But man cannot live on beer alone. He must have some sugar. So we consume 102 pounds of sugar per person while the rest of the world eats 43 pounds; paper, 617 pounds and the rest of the world 72 pounds; steel, 1,400 pounds and Russia 950 pounds.

This gets exhausting if you take it seriously. You get up in the morning and say, "My, what a beautiful day it is in Chicago. But I've got to get busy. I must consume a pint of beer, ⅓ pound of sugar, 2 pounds of paper, 4 pounds of steel," and so on.

Why are we such an energetic people? How do you account for the fact that 6 percent of the world's people produce and consume 26 percent of the world's goods and services?

No, it is not natural resources. The Good Lord gave the rest of the world a lot of natural resources too. In fact, we are short on copper, iron ore, petroleum, tin, bauxite, and almost everything else except agricultural products.

It may be that the old puritan ethics that prescribed "A day's work for a day's pay" and "He who doesn't work doesn't eat" may have had something to do with the development of our present affluence. I refer to this as the "old" puritan ethics because we now seem to have accepted the proposition that every man is entitled to eat regardless of whether he prefers to work.

The profit motive, no doubt, has been a big factor in our high productivity. This is a country where any person can get ahead by brawn or brain or both. Ability has always counted here far more than station of birth. In short, this is a land where each person has an opportunity to determine his own standard of living and his own level of wealth. Some take advantage of it. Some don't.

One noted observer stated that in his opinion we are so affluent in the United States because the government started interfering with the free enterprise system later in history than was the case in other countries. I, too, think this has a lot to do with our current affluence.

In my opinion the primary reason we are so affluent in the United States is that, for most of the time during our 200 years of independence, we have had a fairly good distribution of the fruits of our production among the three elements of production, namely, management, labor, and capital. Without any one of these our production will collapse. This is elementary economics. If we want to continue having more and more of the good things of life, like autos, TVs, telephones, for more and more of our population, it is essential that we reward management for doing a good job, that we reward labor for its efforts, and that we reward the investor for the use of his capital. In this country every laborer has an opportunity to become a capitalist by spending less than he earns and investing the difference. He can become a small capitalist or a big, rich, powerful capitalist depending on his goals and his success in attaining them. Many of the rich capitalists I know today used to be laborers, and some still are.

Although we in the United States enjoy the highest standard of living ever attained for the greatest number of people, we have a sizable group of people dedicated to the destruction of the system that has produced this phenomenal standard of living—a destruction they seek to accomplish either through violent overthrow or through gradually transferring our individual liberties to the gov-

69

ernment. Why? I do not have good answers to this except that, in a society in which competition is so basic to efficiency, there is bound to be a significant percentage of the population that cannot compete. Naturally the losers in a competitive society tend to favor a less competitive system even if it means taking away the opportunity to win. This book is for the winners or, at least, for the people who are anxious to exercise their freedom of choice in the hopes of becoming winners.

We hear a lot of criticism of our system's uneven distribution of its vast output of goods and services. And this is true; we do have an uneven distribution. But we also have a vastly uneven contribution to the output of these goods and services. Distribution has to have some relationship to the contribution, otherwise incentive will fail and we will all be reduced to sharing a smaller whole. The person who works hard and produces more deserves to be rewarded with a greater share of the output than the person who does not work at all. This is an elementary principle, but we seem to be drifting away from it. And this drift is very bothersome to those of us who aspire to above average attainments.

What has all this got to do with getting rich? Everything. In the first place the system that has produced this phenomenal standard of living requires investments, and investment opportunities pave the wide road to riches. Capital, I repeat, is one of the three elements of production, and investors are the ones who provide the capital. The Harris Bank, for example, has 4,100 employees and $376 million in capital. This works out to almost $92,000 in capital per employee. Very few employees can or do provide their share of this capital. Yet, without the capital, the employees would be totally ineffective in this business. The usual manufacturing plant requires from $25,000 to $40,000 in capital to sustain each employee. Here again few employees who work in manufacturing plants are able to provide their share of the required capital. So without investors, either big or small, the system that has worked so well for us will be in for a big change. Any worker who spends less than he earns and provides some of the required capital is doing double duty in contributing to our high standard of living, and he clearly deserves to be rewarded. Let's hope your contribution and reward will be sufficient to make you rich, just as thousands of others have already become rich through this same formula.

The mere size of our economy creates enormous demands for capital and, thus, opportunities for investments that might make you rich. But it is the change that is constantly taking place in the economy that enables some investors to do much better than others. The person who is able to anticipate the trend of forthcoming changes and arrange his investments accordingly is likely to attain the greatest wealth. Again I repeat, the opportunities are phenomenal and are available to all of us who spend less than we earn and invest the difference effectively.

The Magic of Compound Interest

Some of you by now will have concluded that I have beaten the stock market to death or that it is too confusing, too complicated, too uncertain, and takes more time and attention than you have to spare. You are simply too busy pursuing your career or profession and do not have the time, interest, or talents to get involved in managing real estate or your own business or in selecting the right stocks. You want a systematic, well organized, worry free, sure thing that will make you rich. And you have plenty of time and patience to do it.

A savings account, then, is your best bet. If you get started early enough, the compounding of interest rates will do it for you.

This is slow and plodding, but is the surest of all ways to become rich. It is available to all of us regardless of natural abilities or educational attainment. The average age of all the people in the United States is 30.2 years. Suppose you are about the national average, say 30, and you have a job—any kind of a job that provides a regular paycheck. You decide that by cutting expenses here and there you can save $1,000 per year. So you save diligently for one year and on your thirty-first birthday you put your $1,000 in a bank savings account that pays 5 percent interest, and you do this each year on your birthday until you are ready to retire at age 65.

By the time you are sixty-five years old you will have actually deposited $34,000 in your account. That is not enough to make you feel rich. But the bank will have paid you $57,734.56 in interest on your savings at 5 percent compounded continuously as banks do today, so you will then have $91,734.56. Is that enough to make you feel rich? For some people, yes. For others, no. If this is not enough to make you feel rich, then you should save $2,000 per year, and you will have $183,469.12. Three thousand dollars per year will produce $275,203.68. Somewhere this gets big enough to make everyone who does it feel rich.

Suppose you are a child wonder, and you catch onto the magic of compound interest by age twenty. You have really got it made because the longer you have for the compounding to work for you, the more dramatic the results will be. If you start this program at age twenty, you will have saved $44,000 by the time you are ready to retire at sixty-five. The savings institution will have paid you $164,546.21 in interest at 5 percent, so your total amount in the bank will be $208,546.21. Two thousand dollars a year will produce $417,092.42. Three thousand dollars will provide $625,638.63.

The above calculations are based on an interest rate of 5 percent, compounded continuously, and assumes that you deposit your $1,000, $2,000, or $3,000 all at one time each year. A much better way to do this is by making an allotment from your salary of $83.34 per month directly to your bank savings account or savings and loan account. This way you never see the money, and you thus avoid letting it get built into your standard of living. It also strengthens your discipline to get it done. You don't have to make a decision each month or each year whether to skip a deposit. Finally, you will earn more interest on your deposits because you will be adding to your account earlier in the year.

If you make an allotment of $83.34 from your pay check starting on you thirtieth birthday and monthly thereafter, by the time you reach sixty-five you will have $96,797.81 in your account at 5 percent compounded continuously. Two thousand dollars per year on the same monthly arrangement would produce $193,595.62, and $3,000 will produce $290,393.43.

All of this talk about 5 percent interest rates sounds rather silly after those 15 percent plus rates we were recently getting from money market funds and bank C.D.s doesn't it? We will never see 5 percent rates again, will we? Who knows. Over the past 40 years savings account rates have averaged 2.9 percent.

Future interest rates will depend on future inflation rates. If inflation goes to 100 percent anually then interest rates will go to 100 percent plus. Interest rates invariably lag the inflation rate both on the way up and on the way down. From 1974 through 1980 interest rates lagged the rise in inflation so badly that savers actually got a negative return on their savings. When inflation dropped sharply in 1981 and 1982, interest rates lagged on the down side. During this period savers collected the highest real return on record, i.e., the difference between the interest rate and the inflation rate. Over the past 100 years the real earnings on savings have averaged from 2.5 percent to 3.5 percent. Any higher interest rates have simply reflected anticipated higher inflation rates. You can easily adjust your expectations up or down from the 5 percent used above.

Let's assume the current savings certificate rate of $7^{1}/_{4}$ percent remain available for the next thirty-five years. The purchase of a $1,000 certificate every January 2 and reinvestment of all interest would produce a total of $166,556.60 at the end of the thirty-five year period. Two thousand dollars per year under this plan would produce $333,113.20, and $3,000 would produce $499,669.80. At age 20 the same plan would produce a total of $359,119.33 with $1,000 savings per year, $718,238.66 with savings of $2,000, and $1,177,357.99 with savings of $3,000. Phenomenal, isn't it? And any frugal person can do it if he has the discipline to do so.

But you are saying that this is all before taxes. And it is. For this to work for you, you will have to pay your taxes out of other earnings and not out of the interest earned. But if the most you can save is $1,000 per year, then you will be in a low tax bracket anyway. If you are in a high tax bracket, then you should be able to save several thousand dollars a year.

There is something new that may be available to you, whereby you can set aside up to $2,000 per year or a maximum of 15 percent of your income *before* taxes. This is the Individual Retirement Act of 1974, usually referred to as IRA. This is available to individuals who receive pay for services rendered (not interest or dividends). These IRA plans are catching on big now with people who qualify. The plan contains a strong discipline in that the money cannot be withdrawn before $59\frac{1}{2}$. It must be withdrawn starting at age 70. Every November and December people are flocking into banks and savings institutions to set up IRA accounts. What these people have in mind is saving taxes now, but what they are going to do is end up twenty or more years hence a lot richer than they would have been otherwise.

Now let's take an extreme case. Suppose a person at age twenty sets up an IRA account with a bank savings department and deposits the maximum $2,000 per year out of his or her pretax earnings until age sixty-five, at which time he or she starts withdrawing the funds. Let's assume an 11 percent interest rate over this period. This person will have $2,845,142 in this account. Unbelievable? That is what forty-five years of compound interest rates will do for you. And this can now be done with pretax earnings.

But it is unrealistic to expect many, if any, twenty-year-olds to start a program like this. They have far more immediate needs in mind, such as getting a college education, getting a car or getting marrried, which means paying for a housing unit with furniture. It is about age thirty that most people are in a position to start accumulating wealth. However, anywhere beyond age 30 is valuable time lost, not only in working the magic of compound interest rates, but in getting assets of any kind, whether real estate or stocks, working for you.

Some of you will be saying that you do not earn enough to permit any savings now. You are thinking that maybe you can start a program when your salary gets higher. If this is your situation, then I have bad news for you. If you cannot save money out of your current $20,000 salary, or your $15,000 salary or $10,000, or $4,000 salary, then you will not be able to save out of your $40,000, or $60,000, or $100,000 salary either. Saving is a matter of discipline, not a matter of how much money you make.

Some of you are saying that inflation will eat up your savings, so why bother? Well, in a sense that may be true. If we have 5 percent a year inflation and you get 5 percent a year interest on your savings, the inflation is simply absorbing the earnings. In thirty-five years your savings of $34,000 plus interest of $57,734.56 for a total of $91,734.56 would have a purchasing power of $34,000. But inflation is an excuse for not saving instead of a good reason for not doing so. If we are going to have 5 percent inflation each year, or any percent you want to choose, you will be a lot better off at age sixty-five if you have accumulated a lot of money than you will be if you do nothing because of your concern about inflation. In fact, inflation hurts poor people far more than it does rich people. So if you are convinced we will always have inflation, you should be even more determined to save your money so you can cope with it better.

In 1980 when we had that horrible double digit inflation, short-term interest rates shot up to 16 percent and more. The people with a lot of money had a heyday collecting those high rates. They at least kept up with inflation. The poor people who had no money to lend at those high rates had to reduce their standard of living even lower. Yes indeed, anticipated inflation is a very strong incentive for smart people to save.

And compound interest is a great way to get rich provided you start early enough in life and exercise the discipline required to stick with it.

Gambling? No

How about the Irish Sweepstakes, the Illinois lottery, horse racing, or Las Vegas as means of getting rich?

I have read in the newspapers of people getting rich this way, but I have never known any of those who made it. They do not seem to set up trust accounts at the Harris Bank.

The odds are so great against your getting rich this way that I have chosen to mark this off as an impractical approach to getting rich. According to *Encyclopedia Britannica,* between 12 and 25 percent (depending on the locale) of the money that is bet at the tracks goes to the state and to the racing association to cover expenses and profits. Therefore, you have to do 12 to 25 percent better than average at the races just to break even. Maybe this is good entertainment, but with odds like that against you, it is a very poor way to try to get rich.

I have never been to Las Vegas. I know nothing about gambling and have absolutely no interest in it. I completely disclaim being an authority on this matter. In an article in *Money* magazine in January 1974, William Bruns, a freelance writer from Los Angeles, discussed the "house edge" or percentage against the gambler that is built into each game. He says the house edge in the game of craps varies from 1.4 to 9 percent, depending on the choices the gambler makes as he plays the game. This means that over a period of time the odds will produce $1.40 to $9.00 for the house for each $100 the gamblers bet. Sure one gambler or even many gamblers may win big, but ultimately, the house wins the house edge. In other words, the gambler must do 1.4 to 9 percent better than average just to break even.

In the game of roulette, Mr. Bruns says, the house edge is inflexibly set at 5.26 percent against the gamblers on every spin of the wheel no matter what combinations are selected. In baccarat the house edge is a rather thin 1.25 percent or $1.25 out of each $100 bet.

Mr. Bruns describes the slot machine as "the most efficient way to get poor quickly in Las Vegas." He says they are unre-

gulated by the state and can be set by the owner to pay off as
frequently or infrequently as he likes. He says slot machines are
not only "a poor bet in the short run, they will clean you out in
the long run." They are adjusted to do just that. The only contest
is how long can you play the machine until your money is all
gone? People who gamble on slot machines know this and yet
they have trouble resisting them.

In short, the whole of Las Vegas or any other gambling mecca
is programmed against you. It has to be that way, otherwise gambling establishments of this type could not survive.

I can't resist at this point repeating a statement my associate,
William Flory, overheard in an airport limousine on his way into
Las Vegas. There were two young ladies seated behind him, and
one said to the other, "I sure hope I break even on this trip because I need the money." Entertainment? Maybe so. Getting
rich? The odds against you are overwhelming. *Dunn's Review*
for December 1974 contained a table showing the "Winner's
Share" for thirteen states that conduct lotteries. They vary from
a high of 51 percent for Delaware to a low of 40 percent for New
York State; most were in the area of 45%. This means you have
to do a whopping 49 to 60 percent better than average just to
break even. You have to believe in miracles to accept odds this
adverse.

How does this compare to investing in common stocks? We
investors never like to see the word "gambling" used in reference to our stock activities, and rightly so. Gambling, as we understand it, is creating a risk where none existed before. Investing
is participating in the ownership of a business that will prosper if
it produces a product or performs a service at a profit. Over the
past forty years, corporate profits have increased at an average of
7.6 percent a year, and this includes a lot of bad economic years
as well as good. Thus, if stocks simply stayed at a constant mul-
tiple of earnings all the time, you would have had to do 7.6 percent worse than average just to break even. Quite a contrast to
gambling, isn't it? This is the kind of odds I like.

CHAPTER VII

You Can Never Get Rich From Your Salary Alone

OF ALL the rich people I have dealt with over the past twenty-five years, not one of them got rich from his or her salary. Salary is important insofar as it determines your standard of living, or to put it in more modern terms, "your lifestyle." There is obviously some type of a natural law that says your cost of living tends to rise to equal the available income. It takes strict discipline to prevent this from happening.

To demonstrate the ineffectiveness of salary in making you richer, I want to use a hypothetical case, except it isn't very hypothetical. This example is essentially what happened to a friend of mine. He was earning $20,000 a year in salary. By living quite frugally he was saving about $5,000 a year, which he was investing in stocks that he hoped would go up and make him richer. Through a series of circumstances, he was suddenly promoted to the presidency of his company at a salary of $100,000 per year. Did his savings bound upward by $80,000 a year along with this salary increase? Not at all. Here is what happened. His income taxes shot up abruptly. He had to dress better now that he was president of the company. The tired old Chevrolet didn't seem appropriate for the president of the company, so he got a Buick and later a Cadillac. All presidents belong to country clubs and downtown clubs, so he had to join some. He had to greatly increase his contributions to his church, his college, the United Fund, and other worthy causes; it isn't good for the image of the

79

company if the president makes only modest contributions. And all the other presidents live on the other side of town so he better move over there too. Of course, homes are much more expensive over there and real estate taxes are much higher.

These same factors applied to the man's wife. She had to dress better once she become the wife of the president, and she needed her own car, so they become a two-car family. She also had to join some clubs, and what do you suppose was the chic topic of conversation at the clubs? Problems everyone was having with maids. She didn't have a maid, but now she needed one.

Such families may begin making a lot more money, doing a lot more exciting things, and creating a much bigger splash in society, but they are not getting much, if any, richer. It is about as hard for a company president to save $5,000 out of his $100,000 salary for investment purposes as it is for one of his managers to save the same amount out of his $20,000 salary.

A few years ago I got a thousand-dollar-a-year surprise raise in salary. At the Harris Bank each employee's salary is reviewed annually on the anniversary date of employment, but sometimes salary increases are granted in the middle of the year if an employee does something meritorious that justifies a raise. It was one of these meritorious raises that I got. When I arrived home from work that night, my family was seated at the kitchen table having supper (dinner to you non-Southerners). I called for attention and asked everyone to listen carefully because I had something important to say. I told them that I had received a thousand dollar raise and that I wanted them to figure out how we could now raise our standard of living by one thousand a year. I knew that this would happen anyway, so why not make a game of it. Our son was fourteen at the time and was totally unaware of everything around him, but this got through to him. He thought of all kinds of things we should do with our $1,000 increase. His final conclusion was that we should get a new car and a poodle to go with it. His idea of real affluence was a new car with a poodle looking out the window.

Unfortunately, too many adults let the fourteen-year-old

type of thinking influence their lifestyle. A thousand dollar increase in salary results in a two, three, or four thousand dollar increase in their living standard. This obviously will not make you richer. It is the sort of thing you must guard against if you hope to get rich.

CHAPTER VIII

Them That's Got Gets

THIS is a term I heard my father use over and over when I was a kid growing up in East Tennessee. I thought he originated it, but I learned later that this was not the case at all. Jesus Christ used this term 2,000 years ago. Matthew 25:29 says, "For unto everyone that hath shall be given." Everytime I read this I think to myself how right He was. Yet I find it presumptuous of me to be emphasizing that Christ was right. It reminds me of the well known story of British Field Marshall Montgomery who gained fame with his success in North Africa in World War II. The story goes that at one time he was addressing his troops and said, "Now as Christ said in the Sermon on the Mountain, . . . and I might add that He was right." That is the way I feel when I find myself pointing out that Christ was right when He said, "For unto everyone that hath shall be given."

Your first $1,000 is hard to get. If you put it in the bank and let it draw interest, your second $1,000 will be a little bit easier to get, but not very much easier. Your first $10,000 is hard to get. The second $10,000 is a little easier. Your first $100,000 is hard to get, your second $100,000 a lot easier. Your first $1,000,000 is very hard to get. Your second $1,000,000 is a snap.

One of our major trust accounts at the Harris Bank was brought before the Trust Investment Committee for review a few years ago. It had a market value of $400 million at the time. The mem-

83

bers of the committee, which included me, sat around the table admiring the account and concluded that no changes in the investments need be made. So the account was put back in the file. A year later when the account was brought before the committee again, it had a market value of $495 million. I do not mean to imply that no one was bothering with this account for a whole year. The account manager and his assistants were working with it almost daily, collecting the income, investing or distributing the cash, and so on. The point is, however, that it simply went up in value $95 million in one year's time without any great effort on the part of anyone.

This is an exaggerated example of what you can do if you have $400 million. This must have been what Christ had in mind when he said, "For unto everyone that hath shall be given." So if you want to participate in this phenomenon, you should get started accumulating something now. You don't have to start with $400 million. You should start on a scale that you can manage. No matter where you start, you will find that the more you have, the easier it is to get more.

People who use the expression "Them that's got gets" invariably do so in a cynical manner. My father was always exercising a degree of cynicism when he used this term. The implication was that those economically privileged were somehow going to take advantage of the rest of us to get even more. But that is not the right way to look at it. "Them that's got" have got it because someone did something that got it for them. The gentleman that accumulated the $400 million trust fund started from nothing. He spent less than he earned and invested the difference in something that went up. He did not spend his time bemoaning the fact that "Them that's got gets," and neither should you. No matter how little you have today, every penny you can save and put in your savings account will be working for you. If you do this long enough those cynics will start pointing to you in an envious manner and saying "Them that's got gets." And that will be a great day for you. Once you get savings accumulated, you can then use whatever management or investment skills you have to make your money work harder for you in things like owning your own business or buying real estate or stocks you think will go up in value. The whole world can be your apple, but it is up to you to get with it and take advantage of the many opportunities our free enterprise system provides all of us.

CHAPTER IX

Where You Live Makes Little or No Difference

WE COUNTRY kids used to think that if we just lived in New York City or Chicago or someplace else, we would certainly make a lot of money and become rich. Later we thought that if our parents had just lived in Rochester, New York, maybe they would have bought some Eastman Kodak or Xerox stock back in the beginning, and that would have made us rich. If they had lived in St. Paul, Minnesota, they probably would have gone to church with Mr. McKnight and would have been so impressed with him that they would have bought some stock in his company, Minnesota Mining & Manufacturing. Certainly if they had just moved to Texas or Oklahoma, they would have found oil on the farm, and we would now be on easy street.

I have concluded that it does not make a great deal of difference where you live. If you are the type who will spend less than you earn and invest the difference in something that will go up in value, you are just as likely to do it in one place as another. In my investment work for the Harris Bank, I travel to small towns and rural areas all over the country, and I find rich people almost everywhere I go. They got rich by staying right where they were and taking advantage of the opportunities that were right there, such as owning the choice real estate in the area, or the local newspaper, or the Chevrolet agency, or the Coca Cola bottling plant, or 1,001 other opportunities that the successful manager invariably converts into a fortune. Sure, there are greater opportunities some places than others, but the people who do not take advantage of the opportunities where they are are likely to be the same people who would not take advantage of the greater opportunities someplace else. There are no shortages of poor people in Rochester, New York, in St. Paul, Minnesota, or in Texas or Oklahoma.

CHAPTER X

Certain Types of People Tend Not To Get Rich

IT IS my observation that people who change jobs frequently tend not to get rich. I have no good explanation for this, but suspect it has to do with their constantly seeking a higher salary. As we have pointed out earlier, salary is not what makes you rich. I do not want to imply that you should never change jobs. Not at all. If you are in a dead-end job, in a hopeless situation, or working for a dishonest employer, or hate your work, of course you should make a change. But if you want to get rich, you should find your spot as early in life as possible and then stay put and make the most of the opportunities where you are. Don't reach age fifty and still be searching for what you want or still grasping for a higher salary. I run across lots of capable and smart people in this situation and find they are invariably in bad financial condition. They have changed jobs every five years and have missed out on building up valuable seniority as well as retirement benefits, and somehow they have not accumulated much in the way of assets.

On the other hand, I meet lots of people who have never earned big salaries, but who found their niche fairly early in life, stayed with it, built up valuable retirement or profit-sharing benefits, managed their modest salary well, and attained beautiful financial wealth as well as security by age fifty.

I think some of our best-known graduate schools and a number of career counseling firms are doing their clients a great disservice in urging them to keep on the move in their attempts to double their salary every five years. What good does it do you to double your salary every five years if you spend it as you go along and reach age fifty all burned out, with no job, no loyalty, no money, no security, and little or no influence? Farfetched? Not at all. People like this are all over the place, and they are wondering what happened to them.

People who frequently move from one location to another also tend not to get rich even though they stay with the same employer. They tend not to take advantage of the opportunities where they are because they plan not to be there long. They frequently do not even own their own home, and as you probably know, investment in a home has been one of the greatest investments most people have made over the past forty years. My wife and I paid $19,500 for our home twenty miles north of Chicago in 1952. In 1983 it would easily sell for $130,000. There is a $110,500 gain we would not have if we had expected to be transferred every three or four years.

This can be a real handicap for career military personnel who want to get rich. They know they are likely to be transferred every few years, and they tend not to invest in local assets of any kind. Sure they build up security with each year of service, but security is not the same as wealth. Wealth is something you can dispose of as you desire. I am not saying that it is impossible for military people to get rich. I am saying it is a lot harder for them to do so because of their handicap in taking advantage of local opportunities. They simply have to be far more resourceful than others to get rich.

To a lesser extent this handicap applies to corporate executives who get transferred frequently. Their best bet is their stock options.

CHAPTER XI

Attitudes Toward Getting Rich Change From One Time To Another

WE HAVE a good customer at the Harris Bank who is worth at least $10 million, maybe more. He tells me that he graduated from the University of Chicago Law School in 1923 and that every member of his class fully expected to get rich. There was, he says, a lot of speculation among the members as to who would make a million dollars first, and almost all of them did make a million or more.

I graduated from Maryville College, Maryville, Tennessee, in 1937, which was in the depths of the Great Depression. There was no discussion whatsoever among my classmates about anybody getting rich. Anyone who had a job of any kind before graduation was a real hero. It was not that we were lacking in the desire to be rich, not at all. There is probably no generation that ever had a greater desire to accumulate wealth of any kind than my generation, the generation of the Great Depression, but getting rich under the circumstances then prevailing seemed so farfetched and unattainable that it was not even considered by my classmates. Mere economic survival was the primary goal. That was a period of great admiration for the employer, any employer. Being an employer required some capital and most of the people we knew at that time had no capital. To be an employer also required a good idea for providing a product or service that someone wanted badly enough to buy. As you probably know, demand was very low then. Desire was high, but demand was low because of the great shortage of money. It was a period of make do or do without if it cost money, any money. People, like college graduates, were anxious to get any kind of a job that might enable them to accumulate enough capital to somehow start their own business and become an employer. There was a strong desire to be an employer, but not with the hopes of getting rich. Survival was the goal. That is the way it was in my world at that time.

The present era is perhaps the easiest time in the history of our nation to get rich. Yet our young people today seem totally uninterested. Our children are in their early twenties now, and their friends who come to our home are about the same age. I visit with them and also overhear their conversations. Among this age group I detect a real revulsion, which started in the late 1960s and perhaps reached a peak in the mid 1970s, against the accumulation of wealth. They think my generation placed far too much emphasis on the accumulation of wealth, and no way, by gum, are they going to spend their lives being a slave to this process. The accumulation of wealth is near the bottom of their priorities. They demonstrate this revulsion in many ways, but most obviously with their sloppy dress and unkempt appearance.

Perhaps this is a simple revolt against our modern-day affluence. I keep thinking that when they get older and more mature, they will be more appreciative of the convenience that wealth provides.

But wait a minute, I also have lots of contact with older and more mature young people, say those in their late twenties and even mid thirties, and they don't seem dedicated to getting rich either. They seem much more dedicated to living it up as they earn it or even before they earn it. I am talking about highly capable, intelligent, and extremely well-paid and well-educated people. Their preoccupation seems to be the level of their current salary, not the level of their net worth. They are constantly grousing about not being able to save money because their pay isn't high enough. Horsefeathers. What they are really saying is that their employer can't pay them more than they can spend. They don't save because they don't have the discipline to save, not because they don't make enough in salary.

I frequently hear people in this age level say that it is impossible to save today because of inflation. I hear this from all age groups, but especially from those between thirty and forty-five. These people include senior vice-presidents, vice-presidents, and assistant vice-presidents at the Harris Bank as well as some nonofficer personnel. In fact, I hear this more frequently from high-paid officers than I do from lower-paid nonofficers.

Well, what about this? Is it harder to save money now because of inflation than it was in prior years? My guess would be that 999 people out of 1,000 would answer this question, yes. But the Department of Commerce figures say just the opposite. The Consumer Price Index, the most usual measure of inflation, has gone up over the past thirty years less than half as fast as the growth in per capita disposable income. From 1946 through 1982 the Consumer Price Index went up 246 percent. During this same period, disposable income per capita went up 447 percent. Thus, it is almost twice as easy for the average American to save money today than it was in 1946. If this is not true in your case, then for some reason peculiar to your circumstances you are in the below-average category. You are helping keep the average per capita disposable income down.

But many of you were not even born in 1946. What about the ease of saving money now relative to other periods. In the following graph the Consumer Price Index and disposable income per capita are plotted on a semilog scale with 1930 equal to zero.

Talk about a hard time to save money! The period from 1930 through 1935 was really rugged in spite of the severe price deflation we had during that period. The graph shows that disposable income per capita went down even more than prices. It was not until 1939 that disposable per capita income went up decisively and stayed up more than the Consumer Price Index.

Sure, it is easier for the average American to save at some

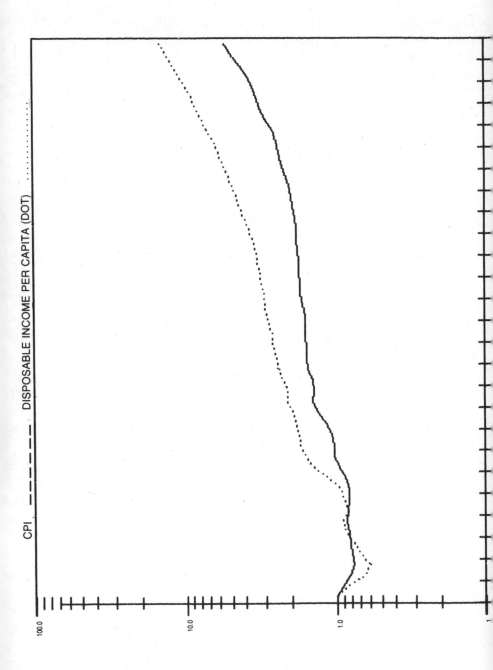

CPI ⎯ ⎯ ⎯ DISPOSABLE INCOME PER CAPITA (DOT) ....

100.0

10.0

1.0

times than it is at other times; the distance between the two lines on the graph shows this. Even so, the average American has never had it easier for saving or spending, whichever constitutes his priorities, than he does now.

Perhaps a definition of "disposable income per capita" is in order. "Disposable income" means the income from all sources, including salary, dividends, and interest, you have left after paying income taxes—the income in which you have some discretion as to what you do with it. "Per capita" simply means that the figure has been determined by dividing the total disposable income by the total number of people (men, women, and children) in the United States.

Why do most people think it is harder to save now than ever before when just the opposite is true? For one thing, the present always seems like a difficult time to make ends meet. We always look back and say things were easier or better back then. For another, our wants are probably the greatest now that they have ever been. Young people today want to start out where their parents left off. This means a bigger and better house than their parents had, a more exciting car, and so on. Never mind that it took the parents twenty years or more to get to that point. Thus, as bad as inflation is, I would have to conclude from the comparison of the cost of living index to the growth in disposable income per capita that it is our lifestyle and not inflation that is making it seem harder than ever to save money today.

I do not mean to be preachy about this. But I do want to emphasize that this has everything to do with your getting rich. If you are spending your time worrying about your present salary level, and grousing because it isn't more than you are able to spend, or complaining that inflation is making it impossible for you to save, then you are not on the road to getting rich. And that seems to be the prevailing mood of our younger people.

CHAPTER XII

You Don't Have To Be Educated To Get Rich

SOME OF the best-educated people I know, lawyers, doctors, teachers, and scientific geniuses of all kinds, do the poorest job imaginable in managing their personal affairs. I repeat, some of them, not all. On the other hand, we have some multimillionaire customers in our trust department who have little or no education and make no pretense of being brilliant or even smart. They have simply spent less than they earned and invested the difference in something that went up and made them rich.

It may actually be harder for the well-educated to save than for the not-so-well educated because the well-educated tend to have broader horizons and more expensive tastes. Sure, they tend to have greater earning power, but if their tastes for expensive vacations, homes, cars, clothing, and the like are even more developed than their earning power, there will be nothing left for investment in things that will make them rich.

So don't spend your time lamenting the fact that you were deprived of educational opportunities and thus have no chance to get ahead in the world. All you have to do is spend less than you earn regardless of how low your earnings are and invest the difference in something that goes up. Then you can hire the smartest of the well educated to serve you.

If you did make it all the way to your Ph.D., don't count on this fact alone to make you rich. There are lots of Ph.D.'s working for relatively uneducated owners. It is not the education alone that will make you rich. It is those investments that do it, and they are just as available to the uneducated as to the educated.

CHAPTER XIII

Anyone Serious About Getting Rich Should Keep Records

FIRST, where does the money go? I am not talking about budgeting, although I have nothing against budgeting. Budgeting never appealed to me, and apparently the very suggestion of budgeting turns most people off. I am talking about knowing what happens to your money. Most people know how much they earn each year because they have to file an income tax return, and this requires that they count it all up. But very few people know where it went. It has always seemed odd to me that General Motors, AT&T, and other multibillion dollar corporations know exactly where the money went, but few heads of families, or even bachelors, have much of an idea what was going on in their personal financial situation. What percentage of your income goes for food, clothing, shelter, education, health care, transportation, amusement, insurance, taxes, savings? Is this really the way you want to spend your money? And don't say you can't get by on less for clothing, food, or amusement. Lots of people who earn less than you are getting by on less. What you are really saying is that you can't dress the way you want to dress on less, or you can't eat the way you want to eat on less, or you can't have as much fun as you like on less.

I am assuming here that you do have limited amounts for spending. If this is not the case, then you do not need to be reading this chapter. If this is the case, then the money you spend in

99

one area is not available for spending in another area, or for investing. Let me give you a simple example. In the winter here in northern Illinois, heating the house is a big item. I go around closing closet doors because it takes fuel to heat those closets and that is not the way I want to spend our family money. The money spent heating empty closets is not available for investment in stocks that might go up or for many other more desirable pursuits.

I suspect a lot of you have no shortage of "empty closets" in your life that are draining off your financial resources in a way that is not of your preference. How are these expenditures changing from year to year? Are some of these expenditures getting out of control? Is there some place you should be cutting back? But first you have to find out where your money is going before you can take any effective steps to get your costs under control. So keep a running account of your expenditures each week for a few years. If you are serious about getting rich, you will find it interesting and fun. For most families you will need only these headings: Food, Clothing, Household (mortgage payments, if any, furniture, repairs, and the like), Heat, Water, Electricity, Telephone (or these can all be lumped under Household if you like), Transportation, Education, Amusement, Insurance, Taxes, Health Care, and Miscellaneous.

After you have learned where your money goes and have determined that that is the way you want to spend it, then you should break your costs down to a meaningful level, like per day, per hour, and per minute. Do you know what it costs your family per minute to live the way you now live? In 1982 it cost my family $49 per day, $2.04 per hour, and 3.4 cents per minute around the clock, Saturdays, Sundays, holidays, daylight and dark, all included. This excludes federal and Illinois income taxes (which is a function of how much you earn, not how much you spend), and charitable contributions.

Why do you need to know where your money goes? For one reason, you need to make sure you are earning more than you spend. For another, it will eliminate boredom for you if you take

100

it seriously. You get up in the morning and think to yourself, "What a dumb day this is. How am I going to get through this stupid day? But wait a minute. It is going to cost me $49 to get through this day. I can't afford to have a dull day at that price. I had better make something out of this day." You will develop into a more exciting person day in and day out.

Another type of record you should keep is an annual inventory of your net worth. If your net worth does not go up each year you are slipping behind because you are a year older and have one less year to go. February 1 of each year tends to be a good time to take this inventory. January 1 would be the logical time, but it doesn't work out that way. On January 1 you are still involved in the holidays and have too many other things on your mind. Also, the Christmas bills have not yet been paid, so it is too hard to know exactly what you have. By February 1 you should have all your bills in hand, if not paid, and you should be in a serious mood for getting down to business with some renewed determination to get your expenses under control.

In taking this inventory be sure that you do not kid yourself. Include only cash and those things that will be converted to cash eventually, such as money in the bank, value of house (minus mortgage, if any), market value of stocks and bonds, cash value of life insurance policies. Do not include ordinary household furniture (there may be some exceptions to this), autos, clothing, and so on. If you buy a new car, refrigerator, or suit of clothes, mark it down to zero, since that is what you are likely to get for it eventually.

What will this do for you? For one thing, it will let you know each year how much progress you are making toward getting richer. For another, it will influence your spending habits if you are serious about getting rich. Let me use another simple example. A few years ago I was invited to speak at the Sustaining Members of the Junior League here in Chicago on "How to Get Rich and Stay Rich." The Sustaining Members of the Junior League is the next step up from the Junior League. When members of the Junior League reach age forty, they are no longer

101

considered "juniors," so they have to drop out. They can then join the Sustaining Members of the Junior League.

The Sustaining Members of the Junior League is a strong organization in Chicago. They have their own Chapter House here on the Near North Side. They have a big membership of active, attractive, and vibrant ladies. It was quite an honor for me to be invited to address this choice group of ladies.

One of our neighbors is a member of this group. She thought it would be nice to surprise me by having my wife, Grace, attend. When my wife gets invited to something special like this, her first reaction always is that she doesn't have a thing to wear. So she must get something to wear.

The Sustaining Members have a rather unique system for their speakers. The speaker does not mingle with the crowd before the meeting as is usually the case. Instead, he is put in a little room off to the side of the stage and given a cup of coffee. He can sit there and sip his coffee and sort of meditate on his speech while the members are holding their business meeting or whatever else it is they do.

When my time came, I walked out on the stage, and there sat my wife in the fourth row dressed in a beautiful new red suit. I am sure that whole room full of ladies were thinking, "My, what an attractive wife Mr. Young has." But not me. You know what entered my mind immediately when I saw my wife? Our net worth just went down about $200.

This is how it will affect your spending habits if you take getting rich seriously. Go to your local hardware store, sports store, or department store, and you will see lots of interesting things. You say to yourself, "Oh look! Can I use that?" The answer is always "Yes." You can use everything you see that you like. But wait a minute. That will reduce my net worth by $20 or $40 or whatever it costs. Do I want it badly enough to reduce my net worth that much? You will find a lot of these answers coming out "No."

CHAPTER XIV

Being Rich Does Not Solve All Your Problems

"THE VERY rich are different from you and me," said F. Scott Fitzgerald.

"Yes," retorted Ernest Hemingway, "they have more money."

And Hemingway was right. They just have more money. The very rich have all the basic problems that the not-so-rich have—problems of health, problems with children, problems with in-laws. You name it, they have it. They even have some problems peculiar to the rich, such as worrying about losing what they have, being kidnapped for ransom, harrassed by baseless lawsuits, or oversolicited for good causes.

I got on the elevator at the Harris Bank recently to go to the employee's cafeteria for coffee. There were two young girls on the elevator. One was saying to the other, "My grandmother said that if she could afford it, she would have a nervous breakdown."

But if you are going to have problems anyway, it is much better that you be rich. If you are rich, everyone wants to help you. If you are poor and overburdened with problems, you are likely to find yourself all alone.

CHAPTER XV

Adversity Creates Opportunity

SOME people are overwhelmed by adversity in their personal lives and are completely done in by it. Others seem to grow in strength of character and spiritual values as a result of personal tragedy.

The same is true in financial areas, especially in the case of widespread adversity. One investor's loss tends to be another's gain. We have a number of customers at the Harris Bank who are multimillionaires today because of the Great Depression of the 1930's. We tend to think that everybody lost everything in the Depression. Many good people did lose everything they had, but while they were losing all, some other good people were picking up the pieces, and the pieces made them rich.

I have been trying to determine why it was that some lost all while others got rich from that particular adversity. Was it a sinister plot of those who got rich to take all from the losers? I find no indication that that was the case at all. Was it the well educated who gained, and the uneducated who lost? No, not at all. The one consistent thread that I find common to the winners was the fact that they were not in debt when the collapse came. Conversely, the losers were loaded with debt or at least had more debt than they were able to cope with under these adverse conditions. The winners I know didn't even have a mortgage on their home. This apparently freed them from the overwhelming burden of meeting debt payments under those adverse conditions and enabled them to pick up the pieces at very distressed prices because those who could not meet their debt obligations had no choice but to sell at any price.

I do not mean to imply that all the people who had no debts were able to get rich out of the Great Depression. Not at all. There were lots of people who had nothing, including no debts, going into the Depression and had nothing coming out of it. Nor do I mean to imply that everyone who had debts at the beginning of the Depression lost everything. There may have been some who were loaded with debt and still survived, but I do not know of any. What I am saying is that all the rich people I know who got rich because of the Great Depression had no debts when the Depression began.

Obviously, it took more than the adversity created by the Depression to get rich from it. It also took courage, foresight, judgment, and the other things that people who make money tend to have. Obviously, also, the person who had courage, foresight, judgment, and all the other things that people who make money tend to have was unable to use these qualities during the great adversity if he was already smothered with debt.

But we do not have to go all the way back to the Great Depression to find financial adversities great enough to create opportunities. Look at the stock market in late 1974—under 600 as measured by the Dow Jones industrial average with thousands of perfectly good stocks on the distressed merchandise counter. This was not a time of financial distress with massive unemployment and banks closed as was the case in the Great Depression. It was a time of record high employment and unprecedented affluence. It was a time of amazing loss of confidence in the future of the country, the world, and the free enterprise system.

During the last three months of 1974, the Dow Jones averages varied from a high of 675 to a low of 578. During that period more than 970 million shares of stock were sold on the New York Stock Exchange. This doesn't include all the millions of shares that were sold on the American Stock Exchange, in the various regional exchanges, and in the Over the Counter Market. On De-

106

cember 7, 1974, the Dow Jones started its sharp climb from the low of 578 to 1004 by December 31, 1976. This means a lot of investors dumped a lot of stocks at what turned out to be distressed prices. But what about the other side of this situation? For every stock sold there has to be a buyer. So a lot of buyers obviously took advantage of this period of financial adversity to buy a lot of stocks at the same distressed prices. Somebody somewhere made a lot of money by taking advantage of the opportunity created by the adversity of the 1974 stock market collapse.

The adversities we have been talking about are broad scale national affairs that tend to affect everyone one way or another. What about private personal adversities? Is there anything to be gained from such experience? Yes, indeed, if the individual is able to gain in strength, stature, character, and humility from it. R. H. Macy went broke six times before he succeeded with his department store. Milton Hershey went broke twice before he succeeded in the candy business. As I look back over my long life, I recognize that my greatest disappointments in love, career, finance, and even health have turned out to be blessings in disguise. At age forty-eight I discovered I had a cataract. What a humbling experience this was. And at what I thought was such a young age. Your first reaction is likely to be anger. Why me, with all of my great plans? This is followed by humility resulting from the realization that you are not all-powerful, that there are things clearly beyond your control. It gives you a much greater understanding of the other guy's problems. You realize that some people are blind. In short, a personal adversity of this type, if you are able to cope with it, is likely to make you a better person and better able to serve your employer in spite of your new limitations.

So your favorite stock that you thought was a sure thing went down and stayed down. Does this destroy you as an investor or does it simply bring you back to the realization that you are not infallible? It takes a certain amount of adversity in the stock market to keep your thinking in proper perspective. If all the stocks you buy go up, you are likely to get the idea that you are a wizard. Eventually, you must have enough failures to keep you humble.

Let us take this matter of personal adversities one step further. Should you be in debt? Should you have a mortgage on your home? Should you pay finance charges on your new car, refrigerator, and so on? You get big arguments by smart people on this, especially over home mortgages, because they are subsidized by the tax laws. I have lots of rich friends who maintain big mortgages on their big homes because of the tax break. I read in the paper recently that in 1976 close to one half of the American people "dissaved," that is, they spent more than they earned and thus incurred debt. I know several ambitious young men who live in big houses with big mortgages that they admit are too much for them, but their theory is they will grow into it, meaning their increasing earning power will eventually support this standard of living. Their thinking is, why should they wait until they can afford it when they know their earning power is rising? Why not enjoy the good life now as well as then?

This type of approach is fine if everything does in fact progress on schedule. But any kind of personal adversity could be tragic in these households. There is no room for a disabling auto accident, a heart attack, eye surgery, a nervous breakdown, or a thousand and one other frailties the human body is subject to. In short, this approach is the ultimate in living dangerously, and they are totally unaware of it.

I, personally, do not favor individual, nonbusiness debt of any kind, even for a mortgage on the house. But I am not prepared to argue the point with others. It simply suits my purpose in life and my personality not to be in debt. I guess it all started with me when I was about ten years old. I had earned $15 by picking up chestnuts, which I sold at the store for five cents a pint, putting straw in the furrows, receiving gifts from relatives, and catching rabbits, which sold for ten cents apiece at that time. I lent this $15 to my Grandfather Walker, and he paid me 5 percent interest. I thought this was the greatest thing ever, to get seventy-five cents a year without having to work for it. I concluded at that young age that what I really needed was about ten grandfathers to whom I could lend $15 apiece, I also concluded that I would be a lender, not a borrower, and that has been my approach throughout life. I don't think I have paid more than $100 cumulatively for interest. We have never had a mortgage on our house, and that has repaid us greatly in peace of mind during all of our adversities, including the collapse of stock prices. I would much rather hold mortgages on all the houses in our block than be paying a mortgage on our home.

I am convinced the people who are able to take advantage of the opportunities that are created by adversities are the people who are not in debt. They are also the people who are most likely to survive adversities.

CHAPTER XVI

Your Lifestyle Would Not Change Much If You Were Rich

WHAT would you do differently if you were rich? I am not talking about what good causes would you donate a lot of money to if you had far more than you needed. We all have favorite charities we would love to support in a big way. I am talking about how you would change your lifestyle if money were no problem. I submit that you would not change very much.

Several years ago a gentleman and his wife came to the Harris to talk to us about managing his money. He had sold his company to a big company and had $2 million cash after paying his income taxes. His wife told me that this was the first time in their thirty years of married life that they had had any money to spend. All those years every penny they could scrapc up had gone into the business to pay for equipment, inventories, or receivables, or to meet the payroll. A bare minimum was taken out for living expenses. Now they had sold the company and had nothing but money.

What were they going to do differently now? I asked the lady if they were going to move to a bigger house. No, she hadn't even thought of it. Why should they? They liked their house, and they liked their neighbors. No, they definitely would not be moving. How about a new car? No, their old Ford was fine. I pressed for something that she must want, now that she had lots of

111

money. She said the only thing she really wanted was an automatic washing machine. She had always wanted one, and when she got back home, she was planning to get one. That doesn't sound like very much for a lady with $2 million in the bank, does it?

The next day I saw the husband rushing through the noonday crowds on LaSalle Street. I stopped him and asked where he was going so fast. He said he had read an ad in the Chicago paper that Mages Sporting Goods Store on West Madison had a sale on golf balls at one dollar per dozen. He was going to load up on them to take home with him on the airplane. Two million dollars in the bank and he was risking missing his flight to load up on dollar-a-dozen golf balls.

Earlier in this book I mentioned the people around Chicago who sold their solid waste disposal business to a publicly traded company in Oak Brook, Illinois, called Waste Management, Inc. I have become well acquainted with a number of these people who now have millions of dollars. Their story tends to be much the same. All the cash they could get hold of for years had gone into the businesses to buy plants and equipment and to pay wages. A minimum had been used for living expenses. Now that they have sold their business and have an abundance of money, they plan no major change in their lifestyles, not even moving to a better neighborhood.

I have thought about this and concluded that if money were not a consideration at all for me, I would do only three things differently: (1) since I hate to drive a car and don't like to fiddle around with parking, I would hire a chauffeur and be picked up and delivered to wherever I was going; (2) I would have clean sheets on my bed every night; and (3) I would have fresh flowers delivered to my house every weekend. I would go to the local florist and tell him not to wait for a call from me, but to fix up a big bouquet of fresh flowers every Friday afternoon and deliver them to my house.

CHAPTER XVII

Staying Rich Is Far More Important Than Getting Rich

ONCE you have made yourself rich, for gosh sakes don't lose it. The inconvenience of going from rich to poor is greater than most people can tolerate. That is the reason they tend to destroy themselves. It is an unusual person who can gracefully make the transition from riches to poverty or even from being rich to modest circumstances.

Another reason why it is so important that you stay rich is that society is intolerant of the person who had it and lost it. A simple example will illustrate this. Suppose there is a nice lady in your community that we will call Mary. Good old Mary never accumulated anything, but she has been a good citizen, always ready to help out where needed. Now Mary's time has come. The neighbors are all saying what a good person she was. The Good Lord was not very generous with her in terms of material possessions, but wasn't she a grand person? Let's all go down and pay our last respects to good old Mary.

Now change this just a little. Suppose good old Mary came into possession of a million dollars somewhere along the way and lost it. Look how this changes the neighbors attitude, "Would you believe that Mary at one time was worth a million dollars and blew it? What a stupid so and so. To heck with her."

How do you stay rich once you get rich? Don't hesitate to seek professional help. Staying rich usually requires an entirely differ-

113

ent approach from that of getting rich. Lots of people know how to make money, but are not gifted at all in the art of preserving it. Frequently, the risk that was involved in making you rich is the same risk that can make you poor again.

Where do you find this professional help? Go see your local trust officer, or investment counsellor, lawyer, accountant, or other knowledgeable person that you have confidence in. They can either help you or direct you to professionals who can. You should select this professional help carefully, making sure that your choice is capable, reliable, responsible, understands your needs, and is working solely in your interest. This will invariably cost you a management fee. Anyone who is working for nothing is probably not working for your sole interest. If he is, then you are imposing on him. Everyone has to get paid one way or another. There is no such thing as a free lunch, or free professional help, for the rich any more than for the poor.

I am reminded of a well-known story that you have probably heard many times involving a fourteen-year-old boy who got a job marking stock quotations on the board in a brokerage house in New York City. This was long before the advent of the automatic boards. I will not use this gentleman's name because I have no way of knowing whether the details of this story are true. After years of writing these stock quotes on the board with a piece of chalk, this boy developed a feel for whether the numbers were going up or down. He did not know what the companies did or what the earnings or dividends per share were, but he sensed that the stock was going up or down, so he would buy long or sell short. At one time he was worth $20 million. When he died in the late 1930s he was more than $400,000 in debt, alone, in a flophouse on Skid Row.

Look what a difference it would have made if he had consulted a professional investment manager. Any competent money manager would have urged him to put at least $1 million of that $20 million in high-grade bonds as storm cellar protection, so he would never be poor again. If he had done that, he would have died surrounded by loving relatives and admiring friends.

I repeat, once you have made yourself rich, by all means salt something away as storm cellar protection so you will stay rich under any and all circumstances, either national adversity or your own personal adversity. The difference between $20 million and $40 million, for example, is insignificant for any individual. The difference between $20 million and $400,000 in debt is tragic.

CHAPTER XVIII

Happiness Begins With . . .

LIFE is just one continuous struggle to feel good about oneself. Any time you can do anything to make anyone more pleased with himself or herself, you are making life easier for that person. Conversely, if you want to make life tough for anyone, you should look for opportunities, no matter how slight or subtle, to say or do something that will make him doubt his own value.

Different things make different people feel good about themselves. For some it is athletic proficiency, for others it is physical beauty, intellectual or scholastic attainment, executive power, political success, or owning an automobile. These things of primary value invariably change with the maturing process of the individual. The things that seem absolutely essential for you to be proud of yourself at age eighteen or thirty will not seem nearly so important at fifty. In fact, the person at fifty who is still clinging to teen-age values is likely to be in real trouble. In spite of the vast array of things that are necessary to make different people feel good about themselves at different stages of chronological or intellectual development, there is one common thread that is required of everyone to produce lasting happiness, and that is good personal financial management. Without this, everything else eventually falls apart.

Let's back up and look at this one day at a time, since that is the way we all live our lives. How long has it been since you got up early in the morning, before sunup, and went out in the country where it was quiet and watched the arrival of a new day. It is truly a remarkable event. Yet it happens every day and has for millions for years. The air feels somehow like it has been laundered. There is usually a low fog because the air temperature varies from that of the ground. The birds are highly active.

You will be aware that an important event is taking place, namely, the birth of a new day. Important things will happen this day all over the world. Babies will be born. Crops will grow. The sun will shine. The rain will fall. There will be production, consumption, investments, successes, failures, and challenges. Commerce and industry will surge ahead in this, another new day. And most important of all is the fact that you are a part of it.

But your participation in this exciting new day will not be pleasant for you unless you are managing your personal finances well. Each day you spend worrying about paying your bills is going to be a lost day. The happiest people I know are those who manage their personal financial affairs well. Sure, some people with loads of money still manage to be very unhappy, but we are not talking about the rich here. Now we are talking about people who want to improve their lot in life, who want to feel good about themselves.

People of all types who do not manage their financial affairs well are invariably unhappy, or else they are totally irresponsible. Each family needs one good money manager. Two are great. None is disaster. It is just a matter of time until disaster arrives and usually takes the form of bickering, bankruptcy, alcoholism, divorce, or suicide.

My family and I live twenty miles north of Chicago along the shore of Lake Michigan in a village called Winnetka, Illinois. Winnetka is inhabited predominately by executives of Chicago's business community. It is frequently mentioned in the press as having the highest or second highest income per capita of any village in the nation. Until a few years ago one of the leading supermarkets in Winnetka had a little sign on each cash register for the guidance of the check-out clerks that said, ''Accept no checks from . . . ." The list usually contained from two to five names. I always leaned over the counter as I was checking out to see whose name was on the list; these names frequently included some well-known business or community leaders. The store does not do this anymore. Maybe they have more sophisticated ways now to avoid bad checks. Maybe they put the sign where curious customers like me can't see it. Or maybe we no longer have people in our village who write bad checks, but I doubt it.

Here were high-paid business executives, making big decisions for their companies, occupying positions of leadership in industry and commerce, and participating in church and community affairs, but they couldn't pay their grocery bills. How tragic! How can you be a good husband, a good father, a good citizen, a good employee when you can't pay your grocery bills?

Is there an easy solution to this type of situation? Yes, indeed. And it can be stated very simply: Always spend less than you earn. This is all you have to do to get along well in this world regardless of how much or how little you earn. If you do this year after year, you will have peace of mind that will enhance your performance on the job, and this will almost certainly increase your salary faster than would otherwise be the case if you spent time worrying about paying bills. So I repeat, the way to get along well in life is to always spend less than you earn. How well you get along depends on how well you manage the difference between what you earn and what you spend. This varies widely from one individual to another. This is what makes the difference between getting rich and just getting along well.

Here is an extreme example of poor management of the difference between what was earned and what was spent. In July 1977 the Chicago newspapers carried an article about a seventy-two-year-old gentleman who had been conned out of his life's savings of $72,000. The article said that two men appeared at his door and identified themselves as water inspectors. They said they had to test his water taps. As he took one man through the house to tamper with the faucets, the other man located the hidden money, and the nice gentleman lost his life's savings.

119

This gentleman had done one thing very well; he had spent less than he earned. But he had not made good use of his savings. Look how much better off he would have been if he had had this $72,000 working for him instead of hiding in his house. A passbook savings account in a bank would have been paying him $3,600 per year at 5 percent interest. He could have been earning up to 7.5 percent ($5,400 per year) in savings certificates. But he said he did not trust banks. Perhaps no one ever explained Treasury Bills to him; they have exactly the same security as the paper dollars he had hidden away and, in addition, would have been providing a good income. I do not mean to be critical of the gentleman for not having his money invested. If he wanted to keep it hidden in his house, that is his business. In a free society like we have he should have been permitted to do so without becoming a victim of vultures. I commend him for spending less than he earned. I think it is tragic that his distrust was such that it prevented him from having his savings work for him.

I am a great believer that it is essential for each saver to utilize his savings in a way that is comfortable for him. The gentleman who did not trust banks probably would never have been happy with his life's savings in a bank savings account. Lots of other people are at the other extreme. They are not happy with more than a minimum amount for emergencies in their savings account. They want their money to work harder for them in things like real estate or common stocks. They are willing to assume a greater risk in the hopes of reaping a greater return. To each his own. Hiding your savings in your mattress, however, will not put the icing on the cake.

Do you know whether you are spending less than you are earning? Again, I would urge you to keep records of all of your expenditures for a year or more to make sure that your expenditures are less than your income. If for any particular year you find that you are spending more than you earn, you should ask yourself if that overspending resulted from nonrecurring expenses or if you are likely to be spending each year more than you are earning? If so, then you should start planning for the disaster that is on its way. Bickering will ruin your day. Bankruptcy gives you a chance to start over, but the scars will always be there. Alcoholism solves nothing. Divorce usually creates more financial problems than it solves. Suicide is final but extreme.

This sounds like I am preaching to you, and I am not qualified as a preacher. What I want you to be able to do is to get up each morning and look out the window at the grass and leaves and trees and sunshine and birds and be glad you are here and able to participate in this great new day. With that in mind I will close this chapter with these final thoughts.

- Happiness is not owning the biggest car on the block if your name is on the "Accept-no-checks-from . . . ." list at the local supermarket.
- Happiness is not even being president of your own company if those people waiting in the reception area are bill collectors.
- Happiness is, or at least begins with, good personal financial management. This is fundamental to feeling good about oneself.

CHAPTER XIX

There Is a Time For Spending

YOU certainly don't want to spend your entire life just getting rich. There is no greater tragedy than to read in the newspaper about a little old lady or little old man living in a cheap rooming house and scrounging food from the garbage bin back of the A&P while at the same time hoarding a huge fortune in the local bank or tucked away in a mattress. That is not what it is all about. That is not what I am talking about here at all. What I am trying to impress upon you is the importance of accumulating your assets as early as possible in life and then having those assets work for you to supplement your other earnings, to take care of you in time of need, or to give you the good life at the time when you need to be living the good life.

"Oh, but I will never need money worse than right now," says the average young man that I talk to today. I have bad news for this young man. There will be a time when he needs money far worse than now, and that time will be when his health fails, his children enter college, or age simply starts slipping up on him. Twenty-five years ago when we moved into our house in Winnetka, Illinois, I was thirty-seven years old. Our next door neighbor was a fine gentleman named Edward Allen who was several years older than I. Mr. Allen's gutters needed cleaning out and his house needed painting, but he said he just didn't have the energy to get up there and do it. I didn't understand this lack of energy at all because I had never had any shortage of energy.

123

I grew up on a farm where physical work was the order of the day, every day. Being tired had never been a problem for me.

Several years later I learned exactly what Mr. Allen was talking about. My energy started dwindling. Now I don't have the energy to get up there and clean out those gutters, and I am very thankful that I have managed my affairs so I don't have to. I need money now to pay for lots of services that I did not mind doing at all when I was younger.

There comes a time when every man needs to look distinguished if he is to feel good about himself. The way to look distinguished is to be distinguished. The way to be distinguished is to be prosperous. This time arrives at different ages for different people but, if at all, not later than age fifty. And when that time arrives for you, other people will notice it. In fact, they will notice it before you do. Your first realization of this will be when it dawns on you that younger people are insisting on calling you ''Mr.'' Waitresses will be giving you noticeably better service because they sense that you are good for a generous tip if you get superior service. You should not disillusion them. Service station attendants, barbers, and even bankers and stockbrokers will treat you with noticeable respect when you reach the "distinguished stage" of your life. You should not have to demand this deference in any way. They will shower it upon you if you are for real. And you can't be for real unless you are prosperous.

By age fifty you should be enjoying that financial independence that gives you an air of self-assurance. It is a great time of life if you have made it financially. By that time your career anxieties should be fairly well settled. You should know whether you are likely to be president of the United States, president of your company, head of your division, or whatever it is your ambitions have settled down to. You should have attained financial independence so that you are not afraid of losing your job or being forced into early retirement. I repeat, fifty and beyond can be the best time of your life if you have managed your affairs well.

But suppose you have not? After fifty can be a continuous

nightmare if you are faced with financial insecurity day after day.

So I am urging you to build your financial security early in life, the earlier the better. I know that lots of young people, and middle-aged people also, think they do not need to sacrifice now for a secure future later because we have Social Security, and if worse comes to worse, there is always Welfare. That is true. The Government will now take care of all who cannot or do not provide for themselves. But are you going to be happy in what can be the best years of your life subsisting on Social Security or Welfare? Not me. I want something better. I want that young waitress to think to herself when I walk in, "Here is a prosperous gentleman who is good for a generous tip if I serve him well." You are not likely to get this extra attention at the time in life when you thrive on extra attention if all you have is your Social Security check. Don't get the impression that I am knocking Social Security. I am not. It is great for those who have nothing more. I want more and have been perfectly willing to make sacrifices early in life so I will have more.

I am convinced that relatively recent, major changes in retirement laws and wage patterns make it far more important now than ever before in our industrial and commercial history that you build your financial security as early in life as possible. The significance of these revolutionary changes for the individual's security do not seem to be widely recognized by the masses of people involved. Let's start with the changes that are resulting from the Employees' Retirement Income Security Act (ERISA) of 1974. This law vests pension rights after as little as five years of service under some plans. This means that if you get fired before you reach retirement age, you will still retain your pension rights based on your covered service. The idea is to protect the individual's pension rights, and this is well and good except that the act is producing some changes in employment practices that were not anticipated. There are many old time employees that management would like to get rid of. Management is made up of human beings, usually with a heart, who don't like the idea of dismissing a faithful employee if it means depriving the employee of retirement benefits. Now that the employee retains his retirement benefits under ERISA, management is much more inclined to lay off employees, even those with many years of service, if they are not as effective as management thinks they should be. This is especially true of highly paid employees. In fact, the higher your pay, the more likely this will happen to you. If management is faced with reducing expenses, a greater saving is clearly attained by laying off a highly paid person than by laying off a low-paid employee. So the higher your salary, the more vulnerable you become.

There is another side to this "funding of retirement benefits" under ERISA that increases instability of employment. It used to be that employees with retirement benefits were quite effectively stuck in their present job regardless of the adequacy of their pay. Management frequently figured that good old Joe who had been with the company a long time couldn't afford to forfeit his retirement benefits by leaving, so his annual salary increase was kept to the minimum level. Now that good old Joe can retain his retirement benefits, he will be much more inclined to change employment if his salary increase is not to his liking. This further aggravates the cycle. The more management pays old Joe to stay put, the more expensive he becomes. The more expensive he becomes, the greater the performance expected of him. Once his performance is disappointing, the more likely management is to let him go. Thus, employment of long-time workers and older people has become much more unstable than has probably ever been the case before, thanks to the Employees' Retirement Income Security Act.

Still another big change that has taken place in employment practices within the past few years also increases the need to accumulate your wealth and assure your security early in life. It used to be that new employees right out of school started out at very modest salaries and worked their way up over the years, so that their greatest earnings were in the last few years of employment. Now the more attractive college graduates are entering the labor force at very high salaries. We have heard of choice stu-

126

dents with MBAs from top schools getting starting salaries above $32,000 a year. Other less gifted or less lucky ones get lower starting salaries, but not much lower. Obviously these inexperienced employees are being paid for their future potential, not their present worth. If the employer decides the future potential is not really that great, then this high-paid employee will be released, or else salary increases will come disappointingly slowly. Future potential can also be reduced or destroyed through no fault of either the employee or the employer by such tragedies as disabling accidents or health failures. In the meantime, the well-paid new employee's standard of living tends to rise fairly promptly to his high salary level—big mortgage, big car, ex-wife, present wife, kids, boats, clubs, the works. This is fine, if everything goes well and the future potential is in fact realized. Otherwise, disaster. In many cases we are probably seeing essentially the reversal of the former practice of low starting salaries that built up with experience. Now we may be seeing some of the highest earning power early in life rather than late in life. Fortunate is the young person who realizes this and arranges his future security accordingly.

Let me make another personal reference here to illustrate the neatness of planning your security as early as possible. I spoke at a Women's Finance Forum in Marquette, Michigan, recently on "How to Get Rich and Stay Rich." At the end of my speech one of the nice ladies had a question. "Mr. Young," she commented, "you said we should spend less than we earn and invest the difference in something that will go up and make us rich. You also said that it cost your family $49 per day, $2.04 per hour, 3.4 cents per minute to live. My husband doesn't even make that much money. How can you expect us to spend less than we earn?" I looked at the lady and said, "When I was your age I didn't make this much either. But I didn't spend this much either. It is not what you make that counts. It is the difference between what you make and what you spend that will do great things for you. In almost every one of the past thirty years I have spent less than I earned and invested the difference in stocks and bonds. Now the mailman brings us more than $49 per day in checks and stuffs them in our mailbox. If my employer fired me today, my family's standard of living would not be greatly diminished.'' She came up later and told me she couldn't wait to get home to talk to her husband. I have often wondered how that conversation went.

One final thought on distinguished wealthy people. The wealthy people I know tend to be mannerly, courteous, kindly, and generous. I am aware that such people have a reputation for arrogance and miserliness, and maybe some of them are that way, but not the ones I have worked with all these years. I have a feeling this bad image has been nurtured by people who do not know many, if any, rich people. Perhaps it has been created by blustering characters who would have you think they are rich when they are not. The rich don't have to bluster their way around. They know they are rich and do not feel any need to prove it by being discourteous to others. In fact, they are more likely to try to avoid being recognized as rich. So when you get rich, don't get the idea that you must develop an arrogance to go with it.

Again, I want to emphasize, as strongly as I possibly can, the importance of attaining your financial independence as early in life as possible so that you will have something to live it up with when you reach that mysterious age when you should be living it up. I know that you only have one time around in this old world and that you should make the most of every day of that three score and ten that is allotted to you. But completing the circle in style should be among the highest of your priorities in making the most of your life.

CHAPTER XX

Questions Frequently Asked the Author

Question: Mr. Young, are you rich?

Answer: This is a question that is invariably in the minds of some of my listeners who hear me speak on the subject of becoming rich. The listeners usually think it is too personal a question to ask, but I think it is a completely appropriate question in view of my strong advocacy of these principles. So I will ask it and answer it.

In answering, I would insist on going back and briefly reviewing the point made in Chapter V (pg. 25), namely, what constitutes being rich varies greatly from one individual to another, depending apparently on economic background, attitude, and living habits.

When I realize how far I have come from that hillside farm that I grew up on in East Tennessee, I sincerely believe the Good Lord should simply take from me all that I have accumulated under this free enterprise system for being so ungrateful as to consider myself anything but rich. Yes, I am rich, and I plan to stay rich.

Question: Mr. Young, at what point in your life did you set your goal to become a millionaire?

Answer: I did not at any time have a goal of being a millionaire. In fact, I was a bit surprised when I discovered I was going to be a millionaire.

Let me back up and tell you how this came about. When I got out of law school at the University of Missouri in 1941, I was 26 years old. I had been broke all of my life. I was so sick and tired of the constant humiliation of always being broke that I resolved that I was never going to be broke again. I figured the way to never be broke again was to keep something back out of each and every pay check I ever got no matter how big or how little that check was.

When I got out of the Navy in 1946 I had $11,000 saved up, including $2,900 that I inherited from my father's estate. I started buying common stocks at that time. There have been very few years since 1946 that I have not added to my stock holdings. Some I bought too high, some very low. Some worked out well, some did not. But year after year I just kept adding to my holdings.

When I was getting ready to retire from the Harris Bank at age 65 I realized my family could live the way we live on the checks the mailman was bringing us. I did not need my employer's monthly retirement check. It was just going to run my income taxes up. So I went to the bank's Personnel Department and asked a gentleman named Tom Parfitt, who had charge of employee benefits, if he could tell me about what I would get if I took my retirement in a lump sum instead of a monthly check. Tom looked at his computer print outs and said, "Fred, it depends on what interest rates are at the time of your retirement, because that is the discount rate we use in determining the current value of your monthly annuity. If interest rates at that time are about the same as now you will get around $300,000, give or take $10,000." I said, "Three hundred thousand dollars! Three hundred thousand dollars! Tom, that will put me over the million dollar mark in assets. That is a great idea."

That night when I got home from work my wife, Gracie, was fixing dinner. She was stirring something in a pan on the stove. I said, "Gracie, how would you like to be married to a millionaire?" She just kept stirring the pan and said, "Who have you got in mind?"

As it turned out, my lump sum payment amounted to $292,000.

I rolled this over into an Individual Retirement Account (IRA) at the Harris Bank. This way I paid no taxes on the lump sum and will not pay taxes on it or the earnings on the account until I start drawing it out at age $70^{1}/_{2}$.

That is how I became a millionaire. I repeat: it was not my goal to be a millionaire. It just happened because of the frugal life we lived.

Question: Mr. Young, I don't have a question for you but I do have a question for Mrs. Young. Mrs. Young, you have been married to this guy for more than 30 years. To have attained the affluence you now have you must have had to live a very disciplined life. My question to you is, was it worth it?

Answer by Grace Young: You are right. I have had to live a disciplined life. However, my economic background is very similar to Fred's. I grew up on a farm in rural Missouri with kerosene lamps and things like that. I never had an opportunity to acquire an expensive taste. Every year that I have been married to Fred we have lived a little better than the year before. Sure, we could have lived in a bigger house, driven a bigger car, dressed better, etc., but how can I say that I have made a big sacrifice when every year has been better than the year before? I do thoroughly enjoy the affluence we now have. Yes indeed, for me it was worth it.

Comment by Fred: This brings up a good point. If your spouse is determined to spend everything you make as you go along, you might as well give up and accept the fact that you are never going to have anything. To attain what we have, you must have the complete and enthusiastic cooperation of your spouse. Otherwise you are just not going to make it. The constant disharmony isn't worth the effort.

Question: Mr. Young, how has becoming a millionaire changed your life? Do you get to associate with a better class of people?

131

Answer: No. We do not associate with any better people now than we did before we became a millionaire. We have the same good old friends, neighbors, and relatives that we have always had. I don't think we have enough money yet to get us into a different social stratum. If we had ten million or one hundred million I suppose we would be drawn or maybe forced into a different social setting.

Your friends tend to be determined by where you live, the church you attend, the clubs you belong to, and where you spend your vacations. We still live in the same house we lived in 30 years ago on Provident Avenue in Winnetka, Illinois. The "old-timers" here in Winnetka tell us that historically Provident Avenue is where the "bank clerks and school teachers" live. In fact, we recently had a repairman in to fix our hot water heater. As he was working he muttered "Provident Avenue. Provident Avenue. That is where the poor people used to live." Well, we like living on Provident Avenue. We like the people that live on Provident Avenue. We still spend our vacations visiting my relatives in Tennessee or Grace's relatives in Kansas. The only club we belong to is The Union League Club of Chicago which is predominately a business club—not a social club.

I can think of two things that have changed in our lifestyle: (1) Our contributions to causes that we believe in have gone up materially; (2) We have no real discussions about major expenditures any more. If Grace or I want to buy a new TV set, refrigerator, car, or go on an expensive trip, we do it without any discussion of the cost. Time was, when we did a lot of soul searching before an expenditure of $100 or more.

Question: By freely admitting that you are a millionaire aren't you just asking for trouble? Burglars are going to be lined up at your house.

Answer: No. Not at all. We don't have anything of real value in our house. Remember, we are investors not consumers. Our investments are in a trust account at the bank.

Burglars love consumers. They usually know what they expect to get when they break into a home. I do sometimes fear that some stupid burglar who doesn't know what he is doing will break into our house. If this happens I can see the headlines in our local paper now. "Young's House Ransacked. Nothing Taken." Wouldn't that be embarrassing?

Question: Mr. Young, you make it sound so easy. Why doesn't everyone do this?

Answer: That is a good question. It is easy. But it takes a lot of discipline. The vast majority of our population simply does not have the required discipline. I had a lot of motivation to better my position in life. Being broke for the first 26 years of my life left a lasting impression on me and gave me a strong incentive to do better.

Most people who try this will go along for a year or two spending less than they earn and then decide that they are not really getting anywhere, that they might as well get a new car, or take a vacation, or something. So they spend their savings, and it is all over. It is very slow at first. But if you spend less than you earn for five years and invest your savings in any of the high yielding investments we have today, it will be obvious to you that you are making real progress. Your income from your investments is becoming significant. Do this for ten years and you will really be in business. Twenty years and you are rolling. Forty years and your investment income is like an avalanche. Ready or not here it comes. My income from investments this year (1983) will be about $120,000. That doesn't include free lunches, book sales, and speaking fees. If I just sat in a rocking chair and looked out the window that is what the income from our investments will be. That is what 40 years of spending less than you earn and investing the difference will do for you. At least, that is what it did for me.

In addition to the lack of discipline, I think there is another reason why so few people do this. That is, a simple lack of re-alization that it is possible to make yourself rich any more. The

133

news media is loaded with bad news. This has been true for the past decade or more. So the more you read or listen to the news, the more likely you are to feel that there is no future for you. But it is not confined to the news media. After my speeches on "How To Get Rich and Stay Rich" older people frequently come up and say to me, "Oh, I feel so sorry for our young people today. With inflation and things the way they are there is no way they can make it." Any young person who gets taken in by all of this negativism is not even likely to try.

The fact of the matter is, millionaires are being created today faster than at any time in history. And much faster than would be accounted for by inflation alone. The latest survey that I have seen by the U.S. Trust Company in New York says one in 416 Americans are now millionaires. That is about 0.25% of our population. So while the vast majority of our population is beating itself on the chest and lamenting that no hope is left, a very small minority is quietly going about the business of getting rich. I am glad I was and still am in that minority. Being solvent is great. Being rich is better.

I do find as I go around the country making speeches on financial management that our younger generation, somewhere around age 18 and under, tend to have a very strong desire to make money. This is in contrast to the actual revolt of this age group ten years or so ago against the accumulation of wealth and is in contrast to the 30 to 40 year old generation of big consumers we now have.

At the end of my speeches mothers frequently come up and want to buy a copy of my book and ask if I will autograph it to her son and would I mind putting something in there about a future millionaire. I always say, "Oh, is he a future millionaire?" The response invariably is, "Mr. Young, you have never seen a kid so determined. He is determined to be rich!" I always ask "How old is he?" Her answer is 14, or 16, or something like that. This happened in York, Pennsylvania; Amarillo, Texas; Lincoln, Nebraska; and Watertown, Wisconsin. I started to think that something was going on with our younger people that we didn't know about. The University of Missouri Alumni Magazine carried a short article on the changed attitudes of freshmen students at the University of Missouri. It said that in 1968 they ran this survey. 1,633 University of Missouri freshmen students participated. In 1968 the number one goal in life was to "develop a meaningful philosophy of life." The 1980 freshman class rated this goal as number six in this order of priorities. The number one goal of the 1980 freshman class was "Financial Well-Being." And it said that the female freshmen rated financial well-being higher than the male freshmen did.

I think this survey just confirms my thinking that we now have a new generation of money grubbers coming along, and this is going to make a big difference in the future outlook for our whole country.

Question: How can a young couple like us get started on an investment program in a significant way?

Answer: I don't know what you mean by a "significant way," but I suspect you mean a "big way." You don't get started in a big way. You get started in a little way, and through persistence you develop it into a big way. The important thing is that you get started. The way to get started is by starting.

Do you have two automobiles? Sell one of them. You can get by with one automobile. Millions of families are getting by with only one auto. Do you take a big vacation every year? Stay home this year and fix up around the house. Use the money you save on the vacation and the money you get from the sale of the car to invest in a high yielding utility common stock. Then use the dividends you get from the stock as a source of funds to buy additional stocks. Don't use your investment income to pay living expenses. If you do that you are not getting anywhere. Be sure to use your dividends to increase your investments. The more dividends you get the more stocks you can buy. The more stocks you buy the more dividends you will get. Keep this up until you are my age and you will have money coming out your ears.

135

Question: You seem to be opposed to personal debt of all kinds. Aren't you being unrealistic to expect young people to pay cash for their first home?

Answer: You are right. I am opposed to personal debts of all kinds, including a mortgage on the house. You are also right that I am being unrealistic about this. But it is awfully nice if you can own your home with no mortgage payments. This frees you up to do other great things with your money.

Keep in mind that I am making a big distinction between personal debts and business debts. If, in your business, you can borrow money at, say, 20% interest and earn 30%, 40%, or 50% on it, of course you should borrow and take advantage of this. This is one of the two ways to have money working for you. But only a small percentage of our population, maybe 5% or 10%, can use borrowed money effectively. The bankruptcy courts are crowded today with smart people who thought they could make money on borrowed money. Unless you are a wizard at using other people's money, you will be better off paying as you go and collecting interest or dividends on your investments.

Question: Isn't it true that most big fortunes have been built on borrowed money?

Answer: I guess so. I keep reading about highly successful people who started their business on a few hundred dollars borrowed from the bank or from their father-in-law. But these people tend to be geniuses of some kind. They probably would have made it big one way or another.

If you are a financial wizard that can take a few thousand dollars of borrowed money and balloon it into a fortune, more power to you. I am all for you. Very few people can do this. In my book and in my speeches I concentrate on things that anybody can do. You wizards don't need my help.

Also, I am not talking about big fortunes. I am talking about improving your lot in life. If one in ten of you end up as millionaires I will be pleased.

Question: You say anyone can get rich who wants to. Would this apply to someone with eight children in parochial school?

Answer: Mr. Joseph P. Kennedy did it with more than eight children. But he was a financial wizard. Not many can do it.

You must keep your priorities straight at all times. The health, care, and education of your children, no matter how many or how few you have, must always be at the very top of your priority list. I will bet you would not take a million dollars for any one of your children. I have heard of people with lots of money who would give millions if they could just bear one child of their own. So keep on doing what you are good at.

Question: Most people save so they can spend later. With inflation the way it is, isn't it better to spend as soon as possible before the prices go up?

Answer: Most people who save do so with the idea of spending later, but you are not most people. You are smarter than most people. You should save now so you can invest now—not spend later. I don't plan to ever spend my savings. My goal is to live on the interest *on the interest* from my savings. When you can do that you will really have it made.

Question: What part did tithing play in your success?

Answer: I have read interesting and inspiring stories of people like Mr. A. A. Hyde of Mentholatum fame and others who dedicated 10% or more of their earnings to the church and prospered mightly thereafter. That is great but was not a part of my approach. I am very aware of Luke 6:38. I grew up in a religious home. We took pride in being children of God, but I kept thinking it would be awfully nice if we had some money, too.

I simply saved as much of my income as I could during those early years and put it to work earning income for me. It was only after I had it made that I became a generous contributor to the church. My minister thinks I still don't give enough. He keeps

137

saying I should "give until it hurts." I keep telling him that I don't think his program is that good.

Question: Did you set a goal to save a certain percentage, like 10%, of your income?

Answer: No, I did not. I guess I was in a bigger hurry than that. I simply saved every penny I could every day, week, month, and year.

My first job when I got out of law school in 1941 was with TVA in Knoxville, Tennessee, at $105 per month. That is $1,260 per year. Ten percent of that would have been pretty slow, wouldn't it? During my five years in the Navy in World War II, I earned from $21 a month as an Apprentice Seaman to $230 per month as a Lieutenant. Ten percent of that would have been slow. When I got out of the Navy in 1946 I got a job with the Veterans Administration at $3,300 per year. Five years later I was making $7,600 with the VA, but then got a job at the Harris Bank at $4,500 a year. One year later I got a raise of $300 per year bringing me to $4,800 annually. You can see from this that I had to save a lot more than 10% of my salary. I guess with the good salaries we have today our young people can get ahead fast on a mere 10% savings. Even so, you should save a lot more than 10% of your salary and push ahead much faster.

During the five years that Grace worked when we were first married, we lived on her salary and saved and invested all of my salary. This was from 1947 to mid 1952. Her top salary was $300 a month ($3,600 a year). That gave us our big boost. That is the way we paid cash for our first (and only) house.

If you need the discipline of saving 10%, or 5%, or 20%, or any other percent of your salary, more power to you. By all means do what is possible for you. That will keep you solvent if not make you rich.

Question: What do you do about pressures from your friends to spend more than you want to spend?

Answer: This is a good point. I guess this is called "peer group pressure." It is also called "keeping up with the Joneses." And it applies at all ages and all economic levels. There are areas around Chicago and most other big cities where you are not supposed to live unless you have a maid and use a yard service. No matter how much you enjoy working up a sweat mowing your own lawn, this just isn't done. You will be ostracized by your neighbors if you do. Also, whether you want a maid or not, you must have one to be accepted by your neighbors.

This sort of thing applies in varying degrees throughout our social structure. It tends to show up in the type of home we live in, the make of car we drive, the country clubs we belong to, the schools we send our children to, and on and on.

If keeping up with the Joneses is your goal in life, then you can look at your own situation and know very well what you have to do to maintain your position. If getting rich is your goal then you should never under any circumstances let anyone else set your living standards. You should control your own destiny even if it means not being invited to the "in" party of the year. Just keep in mind that the size of the trust account you build will ultimately be the envy of your peer group. You will be fully accepted when your trust account is larger than theirs.

Question: What part does gold play in your investments?

Answer: None whatsoever. I am not opposed to gold. I am just not interested in it as an investment and never have been.

I guess my attitude toward gold is influenced by my love for investment income. To me, there is no more beautiful sight on earth than our mailman coming up our steps with a handful of dividend checks he is going to jam into our mailbox. Gold does not pay dividends. Nor do art objects, antiques, diamonds, stamps, comic books, or baseball cards. If something pays neither dividends nor interest I am not interested. But don't let me discourage you. If gold or other collectibles are your thing, more power to you.

Question: Mr. Young, there must be something important besides money.

Answer: Sure, there is. Good health, good friends, good family, good looks. I am sure you can add others. But I am not expert in any of these areas. I only talk about things that I think I have superior insights into, in this case money—getting it, managing it, and keeping it.

Are you acquainted with Dr. Abraham H. Maslow's "Hierarchy of Needs?" He is a fascinating writer and thinker. Dr. Maslow constructed a triangle or pyramid of human wants in their logical order of progression. At the bottom of Maslow's Pyramid is "Survival." That is at the base of all human needs. If you are stranded on a raft in the middle of the Pacific Ocean your number one need at that point is to survive. You are not the least bit interested in what the Dow Jones Average did yesterday or what the prime rate is or whether the Yankees won or lost.

Once your survival is assured, then your wants move up to "Safety." You want protection from the elements and all of the things that might harm you.

Having attained an acceptable degree of safety, then you will want some "Social" contacts. You will need friends, relatives, clubs, church, community, motorcycle gang, fraternity, sorority or something. Some people need more social contacts than others. But everyone has a need to belong.

After social acceptance comes "Self-Esteem." You need to feel good about yourself. And you need the respect and admiration of others.

The ultimate, according to Dr. Maslow, is what he calls "Self-Actualization." He is not completely clear about what that is or if anyone has ever attained it. But this is the ultimate of what you might want yourself to be.

If you are interested in this you should check with your local library under Maslow, Abraham H. Much has been written about his "Hierarchy of Needs."

What you are not familiar with is Young's "Triangle of Finan-

140

cial Needs." At the bottom of my triangle is "Income/Outgo." You have got to get your income exceeding your outgo. Until you attain this you are in the "Survival" stage of your financial needs.

Once your income is exceeding your outgo on a sustained basis, then you are ready for the second state in your financial needs, namely, "Saving/Insurance." I tend to lump these two together. In fact, whole life insurance can be a part of your savings program. Once you have savings and insurance appropriate to your needs, then you are ready to get started on your "Investment" program. Your investments can be in stocks, bonds, real estate, your own business, precious metals, art objects, whatever is your thing.

Once you have built up your investments you should be thinking about a "Will." You have worked hard and saved and accumulated your assets. You are entitled to say what should be done with your assets at your death which, as we all know, is inevitable. I repeat, you should prepare your will when you become financially responsible. There is no point in doing it if you are still insolvent.

The self actualization that Dr. Maslow talks about must be a nice "Trust Account." This is the ultimate in financial attainment. It is also the ultimate in status symbols. When I was a kid growing up in East Tennessee, a person's car was the status symbol. We used to look at a big car and say, "Look at that big car. That guy has got to be rich. You have to be rich to drive a car like that." Then it got so that anyone with any kind of a credit rating could buy the biggest car around. Then a person's home became the status symbol. We used to look at the big house on the hill and say, "Look at that big house. It's on a hill with trees arround it. That guy has got to be rich. You have to be rich to live in a house like that." Now we look at the big house on the hill with trees around it and say, "Wonder where he got his mortgage."

There is no room for anything like that with a trust account. You either have it or you don't have it. If you have really got it you don't have to flaunt it. People will know it. In fact, it is almost impossible to hide the fact that you have money.

141

Yes, there are some things in life that are important besides money, but if you have lots of money those other important things tend to become more attainable and enjoyable.

Question: You say it costs your family $49 a day to live the way you live. How in the world do you get by on $49 a day. That is near the poverty level.

Answer: I will give you a three-part answer to that: (1) That $49 does not include income taxes, neither state nor national. Your income taxes are a function of how much you earn. It has nothing to do with your living expenses. (2) In my case, it includes nothing for interest payments of any kind because I do not pay interest. I collect interest. If you have mortgage or any other interest payments you should, of course, include them in your cost of living. (3) That $49 does not include donations to church, charities, or other good causes. I believe in making generous contributions to things you believe in if you have money. Including it in our living expenses might work as a restraining influence on our generosity.

With these adjustments, $49 a day is quite comfortable for us. We still live frugally but do everything we really want to do.

Question: Mr. Young, I am told that a person cannot get rich today without some kind of tax shelter. What kind of tax shelters have you used?

Answer: I would divide my tax shelter uses into two periods: (1) Before I became a millionaire and (2) after I became a millionaire.

When I was struggling on my way up I paid full taxes all the way. I didn't even have a mortgage on my home, which is the most widely spread tax shelter of all. I did hold a few municipal bonds, but this was not a significant factor in cutting my taxes or increasing my wealth. I was in a 60% tax bracket before I retired. I groused and paid.

I was not against tax shelters, not at all. I just couldn't find one that seemed appropriate for me. The tax shelters that I could afford always seemed to be more like tax losses than tax shelters. The good ones that I found (like tree farming and oil wells) seemed suitable only for the big rich and not for people like me who were struggling to make it.

So I made my first million the hard way, without the use of tax shelters.

But tax shelters are going to be a big factor in my second million. Here are the tax breaks I have now: (1) When I retired from the Harris Bank I took all of my retirement benefits in a lump sum and rolled it over into an Individual Retirement Account (IRA). I paid no taxes at the time and will pay no taxes until I take the money out of the account. I must take it out on an actuarial basis starting at age 70½. (2) Since I am now self employed I have a Keogh Plan. I can, and do, put 15% of earned income (not investment income) or $15,000 a year, whichever is smaller, in this account and pay no taxes on it until I start taking it out at age 70½. (3) I opened a regular IRA account and put $2,000 in it as soon as these accounts became available under the Economic Recovery Tax Act of 1981. I plan to add $2,000 a year out of pretax earnings to this account until I reach age 70½. (4) The electric utility dividend reinvestment plan included in the 1981 Tax Act gives me a $1,500 per year tax deferral. (5) I have increased my holding in tax exempt bonds over the past year or two when those 12% plus yields were available.

All of these sources add up to about $90,000 in tax exempt or tax deferred income for me in 1983. That is great. That makes the second million a lot easier. But these are all recent developments for me. The IRAs, Keogh plans, and utility dividend reinvestment tax breaks were not available to me when I was on my way up.

These new tax breaks make it much easier to get rich than it was before the Tax Act of 1981. Don't neglect the benefits of this Act. It was designed to help little people. The $2,000 per year in an IRA means nothing to the big rich but can mean a pleasant retirement for the rest of us. The $1,500 per year tax break from utility dividend reinvestments is insignificant for the big rich but means a lot to the person who is trying to better his/her position in life.

I don't understand why everyone who qualifies doesn't make use of the IRA. It is absolutely too good a deal to pass up. Yet a relatively small percentage of our workers are using it. The higher the tax bracket you are in, the greater the benefit for you. In my own case, I am in a 50% tax bracket (in spite of all the sheltered income described above). I opened my $2,000 IRA account at the Harris Bank in early February 1982 when the bank was paying 17.25% on 30 month fixed rate CDs for IRA accounts. With my 50% tax rate plus the 17.25% yield I will get 67.25% return on my investment each year for $2^1/_2$ years. How can I beat that?

Yes, you can have a regular $2,000 per year IRA, or $2,250 if you have a non-working spouse or $4,000 if you have a working spouse, in addition to a Keogh Plan. Many people don't seem to realize this.

Yes, you can put more than $2,000 or $2,250 or $4,000 in an IRA under certain circumstances. I did it. There are two parts to the IRA law. One part is what is now widely known as the $2,000, $2,250, or $4,000 per year provision.

The other part that is not well known provides that if you are a participant in a qualified retirement plan and you leave the plan you can "roll over" your interest in the plan into an IRA provided your employer will give you your share in a lump sum. There is no limit on this. You can roll over a billion dollars if you have that much coming to you.

It is up to your employer as to whether you can take your retirement in a lump sum. You cannot demand it. Very few employers will do this now but more and more are coming around to it. The Harris Bank will do it only on a selective basis. I had to convince a management committee of three people that I would always manage my financial affairs in such a way that I would never be an embarrassment to the Harris Bank. Mr. Harris doesn't want a bunch of derelicts around saying they are retired vice presidents of the Harris Bank. It is not good for the image of the bank.

Let me tell you how I invested the $292,000 in my IRA roll over account. I think you will find this interesting. I put most of it in high grade corporate bonds to get the high yield as I don't have to pay taxes on it. I invested it to produce $30,000 a year in tax deferred income. I have reinvested the accumulated earnings so that account now produces $36,500 a year tax deferred income for me. Do you know what $36,500 a year is? It is exactly $100 a day for a 365 day year. Saturdays, Sundays, holidays, $100 a day. I tend to think of this as a beautiful vine that grows right through our living room. Every night at exactly midnight a $100 bill drops off into a basket. At one minute past midnight another $100 bill starts forming very slowly. As the day goes along that $100 gets bigger, bigger, and bigger. At midnight tonight another $100 bill drops into the basket. Isn't that great?

Wouldn't you like to have a vine like this growing through your living room? Well, you can. But you have to do three things to get it. (1) You have to manage your affairs now so you will not need your monthly retirement check when you retire. (2) You have to have an employer who will give you your retirement benefits in a lump sum, and (3) you must keep this money separate from all other assets. If you comingle it with your other assets then you will have to pay the taxes now and you have blown the whole thing. So you must put it in a trust account and the trust company cannot comingle it with other trust assets.

These are the three things you have to do if you want a vine like that growing through your living room when you get to be my age.

Question: What kind of stock should a first time investor buy?

Answer: I always urge a first time investor to choose a very high quality, well known, and conservative stock like AT&T, IBM, Exxon, or something like that. Your first purchase should not be a little known speculative stock. If it goes down it may never come back. An experience like this may turn you against the stock market forever, and the U.S. economy will lose a source of capital. Also, you may lose your incentive to get rich after an early experience like that.

You should start off with a quality stock and get a feel for how it goes down as well as up and also get the thrill of collecting dividends before you venture into the wild speculative world of high risk stocks.

Question: What was the best investment you ever made?

Answer: The house I live in. In 1952 we paid $19,500 for our home. Today, 31 years later, we could easily sell it for $125,000. But we did not buy it as an investment at all. We bought the place because we wanted to live there. It is purely incidental to us that it also turned out to be a good investment.

Question: What is the best stock investment you ever made?

Answer: I guess that would be Peabody Coal in the mid to late 1950s. It looked like Peabody was going broke at the time. They were a big supplier of coal to retail coal yards. The rapid spread of natural gas for home heating was simply crowding coal out of the business. Peabody had skipped the dividends on both its common and preferred stock and the common had collapsed to $3 a share.

The company got a new chief executive officer named Otto Gressens. Mr. Gressens announced publicly that he was going to take the company out of the retail coal business, lay off a lot of employees, move out of expensive rental quarters into a lower rent area, and otherwise cut expenses to the bone. He was then going to concentrate the business of providing coal on long term contracts to the public utilities.

I believed this gentleman could do it, so I bought some stock at 3. It soon dropped to $2^7/_8$. I bought some more. It then raised to $3^1/_8$. I bought more. Then more at $5, $10, $32, and $37 before

146

Kennecott Copper bought the company out at 48½. This one success gave me the reputation among my fellow employees at the Harris Bank as a wizard.

Question: What is the worst investment you ever made?

Answer: I bought stocks in four companies that went bankrupt. I guess those four would tie for my worst investments. Actually that is not quite correct. Three of these companies did not bother to go through bankruptcy. You only go through bankruptcy when there is hope. If there is no hope you just disappear.

I knew at the time that these were high risk ventures and that we could easily lose all of our investment. I also knew that if things went well for us any one of these four ventures could make us rich. Unfortunately, none of the four had that mysterious something that makes the difference between success and failure.

The important thing is that you know the risk you are taking when you make investments like these and satisfy yourself that you want to take that risk.

I have no regrets at all about these losses. They were greatly overshadowed by other successes.

Question: Where can little people like us get help with our investments?

Answer: You can't. You just have to do it yourself. Once you get a lot of money the investment counselors, bank trust departments, and others are anxious to manage your money for a fee. But it is not economical for these professional money managers to handle small accounts. And for them a small account tends to be anything under $500,000.

You can usually get some help from your stockbroker, but keep in mind his primary business is buying and selling stocks, not investment counseling. The final decision should be yours. So don't blame someone else if your stocks go down.

Go to your local library and check out some books on investments. They have lots of them. A good one to start with is Fred Young's book on *How to Get Rich and Stay Rich*. If you are still interested after that, there is a book by Richard K. Rifenbark, *How to Beat the Salary Trap* (McGraw-Hill) that I think is quite good for a beginner. The classic on investments is Benjamin Graham, *The Intelligent Investor* 3rd. ed., 1973 (Harper & Row). This book was originally written in 1949 and is still very fundamental to sound investments. Then if you want to get into something deeper and more profound get a copy of *Winning with Money* by Beryl W. Sprinkel and Robert J. Genetski (Dow-Jones, Irwin).

In addition, you should read the financial pages of your local paper, plus the *Wall Street Journal* and *Forbes Magazine*. It takes lots of reading but you have plenty of time. You have evenings, weekends, holidays, and vacation time.

Don't be afraid of making mistakes. All experienced investors make mistakes from time to time. Always try to learn from your mistakes and hope your successes exceed your mistakes.

One additional possibility. Many local high schools and most community colleges offer evening non-credit courses or seminars on investments. Also, many brokerage houses offer investment seminars, usually for free. These can all be quite helpful.

Question: What do you think of mutual funds?

Answer: If you have no interest, ability, or inclination to pick your own investments, then mutual funds are probably your best bet. But pick a mutual fund that is designed to do what you have in mind. If you want capital appreciation with no regard to current income, then select one that has capital appreciation as its goal. If you want maximum income with safety, then pick one that has as its goal maximum income with safety of principal. They all spell out the purpose of the fund in their prospectus and other materials.

Mutual funds have the big advantage of giving you wide diversification. If you pick one stock and it goes down the drain, your loss is great. If the mutual fund manager picks a bad investment it will be one of many in the portfolio and the loss to you will not be great, unless he picks nothing but losers.

Question: What about your children? Are they as frugal as you are?

Answer: Yes indeed. They are chips off the old block. Of course, they haven't had to be as frugal as I am because they have a rich father, but they know what it is all about.

Our daughter, Betty Young FitzSimons, is married to a Navy pilot. She and John are managing their financial affairs very well. She saved every penny from the day she was born to help pay her college expenses and then went through four years at the University of Mississippi without spending any of her own money. She spent my money and used her $3,600 savings for the down payment on their home.

Our son, Fred III, is now a soil scientist in Alaska. He married Katie Hartley who already owned her home. He is well on his way with a nice holding of stocks and money market funds. Our grandson, Evan Hartley Young, was born February 13, 1982, in time to qualify for the $1,000 distribution of oil revenues the State of Alaska made to each of its residents as of April 1, 1982. He, too, is off to a good start on his first million.